Modernist Escapes

Editorial direction: Anna Godfrey
Copyediting: Aimee Selby
Contributor: Ruth Lang
Picture research assisted by: Cindy Parthonnaud
Design and concept: Stefi Orazi Studio
Production: Andrea Cobré
Separations: Reproline mediateam, Munich
Printing and binding: DZS Grafik, d.o.o., Ljubljana
Paper: 140g Magno Natural

Printed in Slovenia
ISBN 978-3-7913-8634-8
www.prestel.com

Cover: Alastair Philip Wiper

Acknowledgements
The author would like to extend her special thanks to the
owners and institutions of the buildings featured who have
contributed to the realisation of this book. A special thanks
is due to Ruth Lang, David McKendrick, Lucie Roberts and
Damian Wayling, Christoffer Rudquist and the RIBA Library.
The author would also like to express her sincere thanks to
Anna Godfrey, Aimee Selby and the rest of the publishing
team at Prestel.

Modernist Escapes

An Architectural Travel Guide

Stefi Orazi

Prestel
Munich • London • New York

Contents

Introduction

We are surrounded by architecture. However, much of our experience of it is from the outside. One of my first holidays as an adult was a trip to Vienna in the late 1990s. I dragged my sister to the Wiener Werkbundsiedlung, an experimental 1930s housing estate about fifty minutes from the city centre. As we wandered among the houses, designed by the likes of Adolf Loos and Gerrit Rietveld, what I really wanted to do was look inside them. People have long had a fascination with other people's homes, especially those that belonged to creative individuals and are filled with the artefacts of everyday human life. Not only do they make us feel closer to their inhabitants and the times they were living in, we also get a better understanding of the architect who designed them. The general principles of modernism, such as large areas of glazing, orientation towards the sun, and a connection between the inside and the outdoors, are demonstrated in many of the examples featured here, with regional variations. It is in the architects' own homes, however, that we find those principles best expressed. Many of the houses I have chosen — such as the Gropius House in Lincoln, Massachusetts, by Bauhaus founder Walter Gropius, or 2 Willow Road in London, by Hungarian-born Ernő Goldfinger — were designed for the architects' own occupation.

Ever since that trip to Vienna I have included sightseeing of modernist architecture whenever I travel, especially buildings that are open to the public, such as Ludwig Mies van der Rohe's Villa Tugendhat in Brno, Czech Republic, or the Sonneveld House in Rotterdam, Netherlands, by Brinkman & Van der Vlugt. A few years ago, faced with the daunting task of finishing my first book, *Modernist Estates*, I booked a week's stay at the Anderton House in Devon. The house was designed by Peter Aldington in the 1970s and is now owned by the Landmark Trust and available for overnight stays — it was the perfect escape and inspiration to help me to write. A few years later, confronted with a similar deadline, I headed by train to Éveux, near Lyon in France, to stay in Le Corbusier's La Tourette. The Dominican monastery with its tiny rooms (or 'cells'), each equipped with just a desk, a single bed and Charlotte Perriand-designed space-saving cabinet, is run as a hotel, albeit with the caveat that talking is forbidden anywhere except for the refectory. When I returned, a friend told me of Marcel Breuer's Flaine, a jaw-dropping, cliff-hanging ski resort in France, and there began the idea of compiling all these unique places into a book.

Some of the buildings have survived against the odds, whether it be the takeover of the Bauhaus by the Nazis during the Second World War or the seizing of the opulent, Loos-designed Villa Müller by the communist government of Czechoslovakia. Each has a unique story, however. These are the lucky ones, as they have been restored and maintained either by the state, foundations, or organisations such as the National Trust in the UK, or by philanthropic individuals. Others, such as La Ricarda in Barcelona by Antonio Bonet Castellana, have been passed down within the family and are now in the hands of second- or third-generation owners who have chosen to open their homes to the public, often to help fund the high cost of maintaining these frequently experimental structures. By visiting these fascinating and historically important buildings, not only do we gain a unique experience, but we are also helping to protect and secure their future.

How to use this book

The featured buildings are presented in a geographical sequence, so that buildings in the same location are grouped together. English-language place names have been used throughout. Addresses are formatted in the following order: street number, street name, city, county or state (where relevant), postal code, country.

Please note that while every care has been taken to ensure accuracy throughout this book, details are subject to change and it is advisable to check times and access information prior to visiting or arranging travel.

Key to symbols

Day visit

Overnight accommodation

Key to map

Day visit

Overnight accommodation

Day visit and overnight accommodation

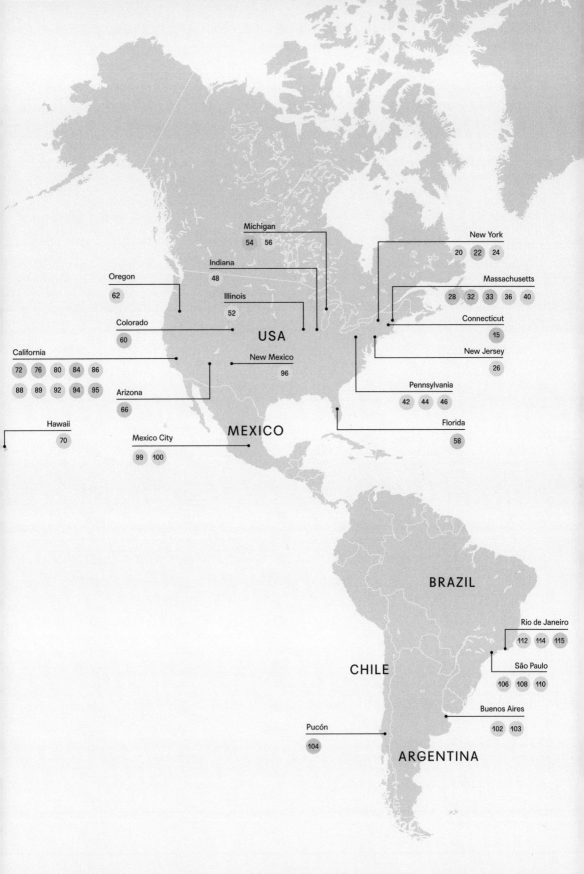

Michigan
54 56

Oregon
62

Indiana
48

Illinois
52

Colorado
60

New York
20 22 24

Massachusetts
28 32 33 36 40

Connecticut
15

New Jersey
26

California
72 76 80 84 86
88 89 92 94 95

New Mexico
96

USA

Arizona
66

Pennsylvania
42 44 46

Florida
58

Hawaii
70

MEXICO

Mexico City
99 100

BRAZIL

Rio de Janeiro
112 114 115

São Paulo
106 108 110

CHILE

Buenos Aires
102 103

Pucón
104

ARGENTINA

FINLAND

Jyväskylä
266

Noormarkku
264

NORWAY

SWEDEN

Tammisaari
270

Helsinki
267

ESTONI

Oslo
260

Delft
186

Copenhagen
256   258

Amsterdam
202   203

Happisburgh
166

Frinton-on-Sea
164

Prickwillow
162

Groet
188

DENMARK

Probstzella
218

Szumin
250

Berlin
206   210

London
170

Utrecht
192   194

Oxford
154

NETHERLANDS

UK

Rotterdam
196   200

GERMANY

Dessau-Rosslau
212   214

POLAND

Goodleigh
152

East Preston
160

Ghent
174

Turnhout
178   180

CZECH
REPUBLIC

Löbau
215

Prague

Isle of Wight
172

Esher
158

BELGIUM

Antwerp
Mechelen
182   176

Pilsen
236

Brno
246

238   240   244

Brest
132

Croix
136

Nancy
134

Paris
Meudon
Poissy
Bazoches-sur-Guyonne

FRANCE

Zurich
220

Ascona
225

AUSTRIA

Payerbach
232

Oberwart
228

SWITZERLAND

119   120   124   125

126   128   130

Corseaux
224

Agra
292

Milan
286

Bologna
293

Éveux
138

Arles
144

Roquebrune-
Cap-Martin
140

Urbino
288   290

Marseille
142

ITALY

Esposende
280

Barcelona
272   276

Flaine
Les Arcs
146   150

Sorrento
282

PORTUGAL

SPAIN

Ibiza
277

Palma de Mallorca
278

Järvenpää

271

Tartu

254

RUSSIA

Moscow

248

Tel Aviv
Zikhron Ya'akov
Rehovot

ISRAEL

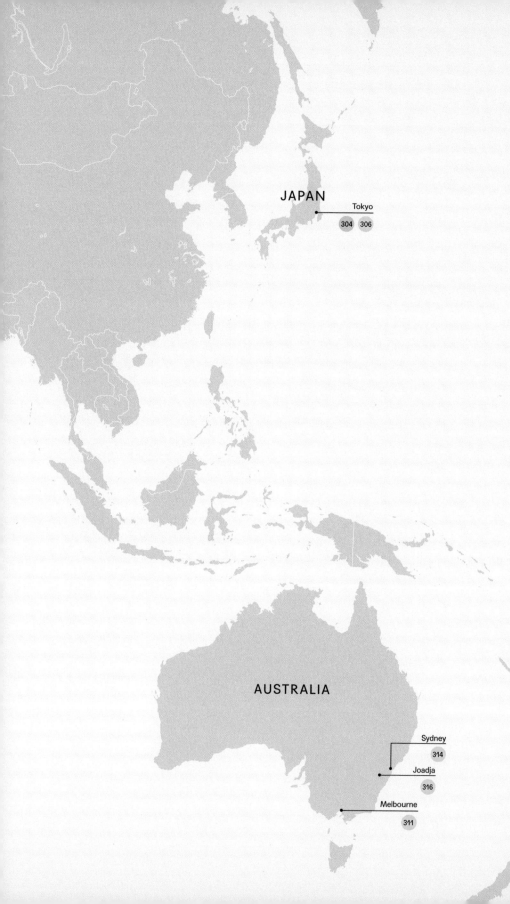

JAPAN

Tokyo
304 306

AUSTRALIA

Sydney
314

Joadja
316

Melbourne
311

USA

Glass House

Architect
Philip Johnson

Year
1949

Location
199 Elm Street
New Canaan
Connecticut 06840
USA

theglasshouse.org

American-born Philip Johnson, an architect, critic, historian and museum director, was one of modern architecture's most influential figures. He described his home in New Canaan, Connecticut, as 'stylistically a mixture of Mies van der Rohe, Malevich, the Parthenon, the English garden, the whole Romantic Movement, the asymmetry of the 19th century'. Despite the various historical references—and undoubted similarities to Mies van der Rohe's Farnsworth House (see page 52)—what is unique about Johnson's estate project, which lasted fifty years, is the sheer extent of it. Plans for the first buildings (the Glass House and the guest accommodation, known as the Brick House) began in 1946 when Johnson purchased a 5-acre plot. It would continue across 47 acres with fourteen separate structures, which include pavilions and follies he described as 'events on the landscape'.

The Glass House itself, completed in 1949, can be seen as a pavilion for viewing nature and for exploring the relationship between architecture and landscape. It is a one-storey building with a rectangular plan measuring 17 by 9.8 metres and enclosed in floor-to-ceiling sheets of glass, anchored in place between black steel piers and stock H-beams. The ceiling height is 3.2 metres, with a full-height door on each facade to emphasise the scale. Inside, the iconic Mies van der Rohe Barcelona chairs, coffee table and leather-cushioned stool are formally arranged on a rug. There are only three divisions in the entire room: a line of 1.8-metre-high cabinets delineating the bedroom area; a row of kitchen cabinets; and a brick cylinder volume housing a bathroom inside and fireplace outside.

Johnson lived in the house until his death in 2005, and since 2007 it has been a National Trust Historic Site. Outside the winter months, various guided tours of the Glass House and wider compound are offered, and even a unique overnight stay for two that includes a dinner for ten guests.

Modulightor Building

Architect

Paul Rudolph

Year

1993

Location
246 East 58th Street
New York City
New York 10022
USA

modulightor.com

The work of American architect Paul Rudolph is characterised by its complicated interplay of space, light and mass. His Yale Art and Architecture Building, completed in 1963, is now widely regarded as one of the best examples of brutalist architecture in the United States. During the 1970s Rudolph's career declined, brought about as brutalism fell out of fashion in favour of postmodernism. Evolving his style, he found commissions abroad, particularly in Asia, where his work remained popular. The Modulightor Building in midtown Manhattan is one of the last projects he completed in the US before his death in 1997.

In 1989 Rudolph purchased a small townhouse at 246 East 58th Street as a headquarters for Modulightor, the lighting firm he co-founded with his close friend and business partner Ernst Wagner in 1976. He transformed the building and gave it a new steel-frame facade, placing the commercial space at street level and adding a pair of duplex rental apartments above. Rudolph initially planned for vertical expansion — the foundations and vertical structure were designed to support twice as many floors — but died before this could be realised. The first phase of the building was completed in 1993 and comprised six storeys. In 2015 Wagner added an additional two-storey duplex above the original rental units, working with the help of Rudolph's original project manager, Mark Squeo, using the architect's drawings as a basis for the design. The duplexes (the lower two combined into Wagner's home, the other used by the Paul Rudolph Heritage Foundation) have roughly the same configuration. The intricately designed interiors with their three-dimensional complexity feature double-height spaces and built-in elements such as sofas and bookcases, as well as many of Rudolph's eclectic possessions.

One of the apartments is available for private tours and event rentals, and all four floors are opened to the public once a month.

TWA Hotel

Architect

Eero Saarinen

Year

1962

Location
JFK Airport
One Idlewild Drive
New York 11430-1962
USA

twahotel.com

In 1954 the Port Authority of New York instituted a plan to expand Idlewild Airport (now JFK Airport) as a 'Terminal City' where every airline would provide its own transit building. Trans World Airlines (TWA) saw this as an opportunity to use architecture to define a distinct identity for the company. At the instigation of its artistic director the firm appointed Finnish-American architect Eero Saarinen, who had won a name for the innovative design of era-defining furniture and reinforced concrete shell structures as part of the campuses of Yale University and MIT. At the time of commissioning, Saarinen's practice had only been established for five years, the architect having worked previously at his father's firm.

The symmetrical wings of the TWA Flight Center lie on the axis of the airport's main arterial road, acting as much as an image as a functional structure. The four self-supporting curved concrete shell segments — covertly but heavily reinforced with steel to give the impression of lightness — flow uninterrupted, with walkways, staircases, departure boards and check-in desks branching off as if part of the same organic structure. As Saarinen stated, 'We wanted the architecture to reveal the terminal not as a static, enclosed place, but as a place of movement and transition.'

The TWA Flight Center was listed as a New York City Landmark in 1994, and in 2005 it was added to the National Register of Historic Places. The concrete structure, however, could not be adapted to accommodate the demands of contemporary air travel and the terminal was closed in 2001. Nearly fifteen years after its closure it was redeveloped, and it reopened as the TWA Hotel in 2019. The refurbished building has retained the original red-carpeted 'flight tubes' that connect it to Terminal 5. Two new wings flanking the original terminal contain a 512-room hotel with a rooftop pool, while a refurbished 1958 Lockheed Starliner propeller aircraft is now a cocktail lounge.

Dragon Rock
House
and Studio

Architect
David
Leavitt

Year
1954

Location
Manitoga
584 Route 9D
Garrison
New York 10524
USA

visitmanitoga.org

In 1942 the industrial designer Russel Wright and his wife Mary purchased an abandoned quarry and logging site in Garrison, one hour's drive north of New York City, and named it Manitoga — a Native American word meaning 'place of great spirit'. Here they hoped to put their theories on informal, modernist living into practice. Wright spent twelve years reappropriating his experience in theatre design by adapting the 75-acre landscape into a scenography of pools, waterfalls and paths, before commissioning David Leavitt to design a house and studio.

The modular black timber structure with its sliding screens and low seating emulates the buildings Wright had seen during his travels in Japan. Leavitt too had spent time in Tokyo, assisting Antonin Raymond in the design of the Reader's Digest Building, the first modernist structure to be built in post-war Japan, and brought his expertise in traditional construction to the design of the house at Manitoga.

Despite the rectilinear, glass-and-timber modernism of the house, nature is introduced in surprising ways. The rocky landscape that surrounds the house, for example, forms a stair to the upper level from the dining area; the doors are of unstripped birch; and rocks and twigs are used to create door handles. A cedar tree trunk forms part of the main structure of the home. The then-innovative green roof helps the house and studio to blend into the landscape when viewed from the surrounding trails. The interior incorporates both pine-embedded plaster and Styrofoam, and features elements designed by Wright that can be flipped or rotated to change the colours in the room from one season to the next. The free-flowing layout of the house allowed the family to make the most of the time and space available to them and to move seamlessly between living, dining and cooking while entertaining guests.

Tours run from May to November with prior reservation.

James Rose Center

Architect

James Rose

Year

1953

Location
506 East Ridgewood Avenue
Ridgewood
New Jersey 07450
USA

jamesrosecenter.org

The landscape architect James Rose adopted an evolving process of improvisation through design and construction, rejecting the Beaux-Arts principles of his Harvard professors. Even the concept model for his house at Ridgewood, New Jersey, was initially made from scraps he found in the battalion headquarters during his posting in Okinawa, Japan, in the Second World War. Rose believed this process of improvisation should also continue throughout the house's inhabitation, and that, similar to the plants that surround it, it should grow and adapt over time as conditions dictate. As he put it, '"finish" is another word for death.' This philosophy also extended to the building products Rose selected, and across the site is evidence of his fascination with repurposing waste materials. He created benches out of old doors, sculptures and fountains from scrap metal, and fencing using railway sleeper offcuts.

While stationed in Okinawa, Rose became inspired by Japanese architecture and gardens. His landscape designs are not exercises in horticulture to be observed from inside but created as experiences, intended to be walked through, touched and inhabited. The former Rose Residence, built in 1953, is situated approximately 30 kilometres from New York and occupies a site only half the size of a tennis court, in deference to the landscaping. Across three buildings it provided residential accommodation for Rose's mother, a guesthouse for his sister and a studio for his own use. The resulting design employs sliding screens and protective loggias to delineate the internal spaces and the garden areas, melding the two into a composition that Rose famously stated is 'neither landscape nor architecture, but both; neither indoors, nor outdoors, but both'.

Self-guided tours are available during the summer months, with guided tours for large and small groups possible with prior appointment.

🛏

Hatch Cottage

Architect
Jack Hall

Year
1960

Location
Bound Brook Island
Wellfleet
Massachusetts 02667
USA

ccmht.org

Cape Cod is home to a cluster of modernist houses built before the 1961 legislation protecting the Cape Cod National Seashore from the post-war building boom. The self-taught architect Jack Hall designed Hatch Cottage in 1960, having worked alongside modernist designers and architects such as George Nelson, Charles and Ray Eames and Serge Chermayeff. Practising locally, Hall developed a sensitivity for the nature of the area's coastline.

At Hatch Cottage, a modular 2-square-metre structural timber grid was raised on concrete feet, allowing the uneven surrounding landscape to continue underneath. Within the overall grid structure Hall inserted a series of three interlocking, flat-roofed geometric forms to enclose the main living space and kitchen, the main bedroom and the guest bedrooms. Open-air walkways separate the rooms and weave through the heart of the building.

Full-height panels of vertical timber boarding, echoing the surrounding dune shacks, can be swung open to allow views out over the bay and form shading for the adjacent open decks, or be closed down protectively against the weather. The east elevation, which faces inland towards the locust trees that shelter the house from the road, contains smaller panels allowing cross-ventilation through the house at high level, exploiting the coastal breeze. As the house was intended as a beach house for occasional use, it is not insulated and uses sliding screens of insect mesh rather than glazed windows. A sculptural wood-burning stove, however, is tucked in the living room between the built-in bookshelves and sofa bench and provides a degree of comfort to prolong evening views out across the water.

The family remained in the cottage until 2008, and it is now owned and managed by the Cape Cod Modern House Trust and available to rent, with accommodation for up to six people.

Weidlinger House

Architect
Paul Weidlinger

Year
1953

Location
54 Valley Road
Wellfleet
Massachusetts 02667
USA

ccmht.org

It was Marcel Breuer who invited Paul Weidlinger, a Budapest-born experimental structural engineer, to build a recreational house in the pine forests of Cape Cod. Weidlinger had previously collaborated with prominent architects including Serge Chermayeff, Josep Lluís Sert and Eero Saarinen. When creating this house for his family Weidlinger embraced the industrial, modular technology he had earlier applied while designing aircraft hangars in Bolivia. Yet he also introduced an element of playfulness in the bright yellow cross-bracing and the 'Breuer blue' window frames, front door and eave details, which celebrate the contrast between the house and its wooded surroundings.

The plan of the house is a rectangular grid plank-and-beam structure raised 3 metres from the ground on timber posts. The overall design is a reinterpretation of the Dom-Ino House principles of Le Corbusier—for whom Weidlinger had worked in France before the Second World War—which enables the wide-span living spaces to be enclosed by non-structural walls. A ramp leading up to the house marks the transition between the wild surroundings and the industrial order embodied by the building. Plywood walls enclose the three bedrooms and bathroom to the north, whereas the open-plan living areas to the south are recessed within the frame's footprint, creating terraces overlooking Higgins Pond. The galley kitchen places all storage below countertop level so as not to obscure the views. Weidlinger was an avid adopter of technological innovations, and despite the domestic setting he installed vinyl flooring, built-in furniture and a surround-sound system in the house. At the heart of the plan, a brick fireplace is set at an angle to the rectilinear structure.

In the 1990s the house became abandoned and was marked for demolition until it was rescued and restored by the Cape Cod Modern House Trust in 2014, and it is now available to rent as a holiday home.

Kugel/Gips House

Architect

Charles Zehnder

Year

1970

Location
188 Long Pond Road
Wellfleet
Massachusetts 02667
USA

ccmht.org

In 1970 the cognitive scientist Peter Kugel was granted rare permission to construct a house on the protected Cape Cod National Seashore, to replace one that had been destroyed by lightning. Kugel commissioned the architect Charles Zehnder to design the new building. Frank Lloyd Wright's aesthetic and conceptual influence can be seen in the nearly forty properties that Zehnder designed in the area, earning him a reputation as one of Cape Cod's most prolific mid-century architects. The design of the Kugel house, with its dramatically cantilevered timber platforms protruding from the steeply sloping woodland, echoes the horizontal planes of Wright's famous Fallingwater.

Zehnder's unusual approach was to build the timber frame of the whole building first and then decide where to insert openings as appropriate to facilitate views specific to the surrounding pine and oak forest, ensuring there are no other houses in sight. The windows he inserted are frameless at the corners, enabling full panoramic vistas across the nearby pond from the living areas, and are supplemented by bubble-shaped plexiglass roof lights.

Internally, the palette of materials is minimal, consisting of the exposed breeze-blocks that form the walls and columns, and timber, used in the beams and built-in furniture and continuing to the clapboarding on the outside. The fireplace at the heart of the living space is the only use of brick. The rooms are divided by sliding doors, enabling the communal living and dining areas, the galley kitchen and the two bedrooms to be linked together fluidly. Although the house appears to be single-storey on approach from the surrounding woodland, the sloping hillside conceals a lower storey containing an additional bedroom and utility spaces, nestled protectively beneath the cantilevered terrace.

The Gips family purchased the property from the Kugels in 1984. It was restored in 2010, and this three-bedroom house is now available to rent during the summer months.

Frelinghuysen Morris House and Studio

Architects

George Sanderson

and

John Butler Swann

Year

1931/1941

Location
92 Hawthorne Street
Lenox
Massachusetts 01240
USA

frelinghuysen.org

Having studied in Paris between the wars, the abstract artist George L. K. Morris returned to New England in the 1930s, keen to recreate the Le Corbusier-designed Paris studio of the painter and writer Amédée Ozenfant. He employed Boston architect and Yale classmate George Sanderson to create a building on the grounds of his parents' country estate in Lenox. The double-height stucco block, with a sawtooth roof light and north wall consisting entirely of window panes, is renowned for being the first modernist building in the region. It strongly contrasted with the cottages of the 1800s and 1900s that dominated the local area, especially as it may at one point have been painted light pink.

A decade later, in 1941, following his marriage to the artist Suzy Frelinghuysen, Morris commissioned local architect John Butler Swann to design a house next to the studio. The predominantly rectilinear, flat-roofed form of the house steps down the slope of the hill from the studio to create a series of terraces and overhangs, punctuated with a curved wall of glass bricks housing a white marble staircase. In contrast to the utilitarian painted concrete of the studio, the residential building has a marble chequerboard floor throughout the lobby and Argentine leather floor tiles in the living room. Although the house is largely devoid of decorative embellishments — in keeping with its modernist aesthetic — the walls were painted by Frelinghuysen with frescoes, trompe l'oeil murals and colours that complemented her Cubist paintings. The couple were collectors as well as artists, and their living spaces are furnished with paintings and furniture by Fernand Léger, Joan Miró, George Nelson and Alvar Aalto.

Since 1998 visitors have been able to explore the house, which retains the original interiors, with hourly guided tours available between June and October.

Gropius House

Architect

Walter Gropius

Year

1938

Location
68 Baker Bridge Road
Lincoln
Massachusetts 01773
USA

historicnewengland.org

After initially fleeing Germany for England, in 1937 Bauhaus founder Walter Gropius and his family uprooted again and headed for Boston, Massachusetts. Here he was given a position at Harvard University, leading the new Graduate School of Design's architecture department. Fortunately, as he did not have much money, the philanthropist Helen Storrow offered him a plot of land in nearby Lincoln on which to design and build himself a family house.

Working initially with fellow Bauhausler Marcel Breuer, Gropius designed a modest building that could also act as a model for his architecture as he began to try and get himself established in a new country. Both architects studied the local building traditions, and the Gropius House adopts much of the vocabulary of a typical New England house—such as off-the-shelf materials and components, a screened porch, fieldstone foundations and a brick chimney—but combines it with distinctively modernist characteristics, including a flat roof and ribbon windows.

The two-storey, white rectangular building sits on a 5.5-acre plot at the top of a hill. The plan of the ground floor is largely open, with the dining, living and study areas on one side of an elegant staircase and the kitchen and maid's rooms on the other. The bedrooms and bathrooms are placed upstairs, with the Gropiuses' daughter Ati's room designed to be independent, having its own spiral staircase down to the garden. Most of the furniture came from the Bauhaus workshops in Germany, including the desk Gropius designed for his office in Weimar in 1922, which is now in Ati's bedroom.

The house, complete with the original interior, is run by Historic New England and can be visited through their well-informed guided tours.

Fallingwater

Architect

Frank Lloyd Wright

Year

1936–39

Location
1491 Mill Run Road
Mill Run
Pennsylvania 15464
USA

fallingwater.org

Fallingwater made the cover of *Time* magazine in January 1938 alongside its architect, Frank Lloyd Wright. However, the iconic image of the floating rectangular reinforced-concrete planes of the terraces, cantilevered out from the cliff face, is only one aspect of the experience of visiting the house. Although the client, Edgar Kaufmann, initially requested that the house in the Bear Run Nature Reserve, 100 kilometres from Pittsburgh, be positioned to allow views of the waterfall, Wright positioned the house over it instead so that the sound of the water filled the residents' day-to-day experience. In order to celebrate the views of the surrounding woodland from the open-plan living spaces, circulation is made through contrastingly dark, narrow passageways.

Wright said that 'The good building makes the landscape more beautiful than it was before the building was built', making the two aspects inseparable in any composition. He sought to merge the landscape with the architecture, so it is both a structure and a form of ornamentation. A continuous floor of stone from a nearby quarry runs through the living room and its two external terrace spaces, one of which leads to an open-tread staircase suspended over a sculptural plunge pool. Like many of Wright's houses, the fireplace is the symbolic heart of the family home. Here, a large boulder from the site is used on the base of the hearth, its organic form acting as a deliberate interruption to the predominantly rectilinear geometry of the rest of the house. Yet within this, Wright also made use of innovations in contemporary materials, including latex rubber and fluorescent lighting.

Since 1964 Fallingwater has been open to the public, and visitors can enjoy hour-long guided tours of the house and grounds. To further the experience one can stay overnight in one of four Wright-designed houses at nearby Polymath Park, half an hour's drive away (franklloydwrightovernight.net).

Alan I W Frank House

Architects

Marcel Breuer

and

Walter Gropius

Year

1938–40

Location
96 East Woodland Road
Pittsburgh
Pennsylvania 15232
USA

thefrankhouse.org

In the late 1930s, having by now completed a few small houses (including their own) in America, Bauhauslers Walter Gropius and Marcel Breuer began to establish their architectural partnership in their new home country. In 1938 they received their biggest commission to date. Following a lecture Gropius gave at Harvard Graduate School of Design, the wealthy industrialist Robert Frank and his wife, Cecelia, were so impressed with the architect that they asked him and Breuer to design them a large modern house for their growing family in Pittsburgh.

The Alan I W Frank House (formerly the Frank House) combines cubic volumes and right angles with organic forms and marked a stylistic departure from their previous work, possibly as a result of having such a large budget. This monumental building encompasses a total of 1,600 square metres and includes five terraces, nine bedrooms and thirteen bathrooms over four levels of living space, a 6-by-12-metre indoor swimming pool and a rooftop dance floor. Advanced features including lifts, air conditioning, built-in projection equipment for a home cinema and internal telephone system were incorporated into the building, most likely at the suggestion of the Franks — correspondence between them and the architects ran to hundreds of pages, with numerous suggestions, instructions and queries. A sweeping curved staircase dominates the interior, and the furnishing includes hundreds of pieces of bespoke furniture and light fittings designed by Breuer, who was responsible for the entire interior.

Today the house is virtually unchanged, making it the most intact and complete example of the Gropius-Breuer partnership. Having been in the Frank family since its completion in 1940, it is now occupied by their son, Alan, who devotes much of his time to the foundation he started in order to preserve the building well into the future. It is open to visitors by appointment, with a donation towards the foundation.

George Nakashima House, Studio and Workshop

Architect

George Nakashima

Year

1946–75

Location
1847 Aquetong Road
New Hope
Pennsylvania 18938
USA

nakashimafoundation.org

The Nakashima complex is a historic artist's compound comprising houses and studio buildings designed and built by George Nakashima. Having trained as an architect, Nakashima started designing furniture while living in New Hope, Pennsylvania. As a reaction to what he saw as the dehumanising nature of mass production, he responded to organic forms in creating his objects rather than emphasising the signature or ego of the designer.

The architect began to buy up parcels of land about 3 kilometres from downtown New Hope, Bucks County, on which to develop his workshop. As his business took off, he added buildings following the Japanese construction principles known as *ki-mon*. The concept, which is aimed at respecting the natural landscape using local materials, shares commonalities with the principles that guided Nakashima's furniture designs.

Combining mid-century modernism with Japanese craft traditions, the design of the buildings increased in complexity over time. Nakashima started with a simple shop in 1946, built from concrete blocks with an asymmetrically pitched corrugated roof. To this he added a timber-framed showroom and a double-height wood store (later reappropriated as a finishing workshop) in the early 1950s. Nakashima also experimented with curved shell structures alongside his daughter, a trained architect, Mira Nakashima. One of the most experimental was the Conoid Studio (pictured opposite), built in 1957–59 using an arched concrete structure onto which was placed an undulating web of reinforcement. He also employed hyperbolic paraboloid roofs to eliminate the necessity for internal structure, both on the lumber sheds and in the design of his 1965 Arts Building.

The Nakashima family still inhabit the houses, but eight studio-related buildings can be explored during monthly tours, pre-booked via the Nakashima Foundation.

Miller House

Architect

Eero Saarinen

Year

1957

Location
506 5th Street
Columbus
Indiana 47201
USA

columbus.in.us

The small Midwestern town of Columbus, Indiana, is home to dozens of modernist buildings by some of the world's best architects, largely thanks to the visionary industrialist and philanthropist J. Irwin Miller. Having turned around the Cummins diesel engine company, his family business, Miller founded the Cummins Foundation in 1954. Working with the city of Columbus, the foundation provided architects' fees for any new buildings that would benefit the community, such as schools, as long as the architects were from the pre-approved list Miller compiled.

Having struck up a close friendship with the architect Eero Saarinen, in 1953 Miller and his wife Xenia commissioned the architect to design a family home for them. Although the single-storey house takes its cues from the glass pavilions such Mies van der Rohe's Farnsworth House (see page 52), Saarinen made it a thoroughly comfortable home, suitable for a family with five children. The house is rectangular in plan, with a grid of cruciform steel columns supporting the roof, which is sliced through with skylights to allow filtered natural light throughout the building. The house is divided into nine zones, with a large sunken conversation pit with a single continuous sofa at the centre and the private spaces wrapping around it. Alexander Girard was responsible for the interior design; working closely with Xenia Miller, he created playful, often personalised textiles and furnishings that gave warmth to the cool marble and travertine walls and floors. Expanses of glazing look out across the geometrically landscaped garden designed by Dan Kiley. This rare combination of an extraordinary client and three designers at the peak of their careers created one of the most important mid-century modern residences in the country.

Following the death of Xenia Miller in 2008, the family donated the Miller House to the Indianapolis Museum of Art, giving access to the public through regular tours.

Farnsworth House

Architect

Ludwig Mies van der Rohe

Year

1945–51

Location
14520 River Road Gate 1
Plano
Illinois 60545
USA

farnsworthhouse.org

The Farnsworth House was commissioned in 1945 by Dr Edith Farnsworth, a single woman in her early forties, as a weekend getaway after she struck up a conversation with the eminent Ludwig Mies van der Rohe at a dinner. She told him about the beautiful plot of land she had bought by the Fox River in Plano, Illinois, about 100 kilometres southwest of Chicago, and when she asked whether he knew of an architect that could design her house, he offered to design it himself. Farnsworth, who clearly admired the successful architect, was overjoyed and gave him free rein on the design. The building, raised on stilts to overcome the flood risk, is constructed of eight external steel columns that support the floor and roof slabs, wrapped in expanses of plate glass. Individual rooms, walls and doors were abolished in the architect's pursuit of simplicity, transparency and purity. The kitchen, two bathrooms and the fireplace comprise a mechanical core within which the services are concealed.

Although Mies van der Rohe and his client had a close relationship initially, Farnsworth later began to get frustrated at the ever-rising costs and the impracticalities of a completely glass home, saying it made her feel 'like a prowling animal, always on the alert'. When the final cost of the building came in at over twice the original budget, she refused to pay the architect's fees and a legal and public battle between the two began.

Reluctantly, Farnsworth moved into the house and used it as her vacation retreat for twenty years. In 1975 it was bought by the British art collector Peter Palumbo, who was the perfect custodian. However, severe flooding in 1996 caused damage that required extensive repairs, and he eventually decided to put it up for auction in 2003. Preservationists, concerned the house would be bought by a developer and moved from its original site, managed to raise funds to buy it, and it is now conserved as a National Historic Landmark and open for guided tours.

Eppstein House

Architect
Frank Lloyd Wright

Year
1953

Location
Hawthorne Drive
The Acres
Galesburg
Michigan 49053
USA

Available to rent via
various sites, including
plansmatter.com

Built for scientists Samuel and Dorothy Eppstein, the Eppstein House is part of a cooperative development designed by Frank Lloyd Wright in 1951 and set out in circular plots over a 72-acre site in Galesburg, Michigan. Of the 21 houses planned, the Eppstein House was one of only four Wright designs to be built there ultimately, although a fifth house designed by Francis 'Will' Willsey, a Frank Lloyd Wright protégé, was added a decade later.

The development, known as The Acres, adopts the Usonian idiom that Wright first used in 1937 and which was intended to bring good-quality housing to America's middle classes as a challenge the catalogue housing that had become increasingly popular in the first half of the twentieth century. The Usonian aesthetic is dominated by large, low roof forms separated from the walls of the house by clerestory windows, over open-plan living spaces. A grid of 3-inch-thick modular structural blocks was assembled using a system of iron rods rather than mortar, to reduce labour costs in construction. These blocks form the structural walls of the houses as well as the central fireplaces. The homes were furnished with bespoke mahogany furniture and fittings to act as natural ornamentation, reducing the need for paint or decoration. Radiant heating is set into the concrete ground-floor slab to maintain the purity of the spaces created.

The Eppstein House was constructed in stages to enable the clients to move in and develop the site over time. The master bedroom and main living spaces are clustered to the north end of the building and open out behind a curved terrace wall. To this they added additional bedrooms overlooking the common land that surrounds the houses.

Beautifully restored to its former glory after twenty years of neglect, the three-bedroom Eppstein House is now available as a holiday home, furnished with original pieces by Wright alongside other furniture and artworks of the period.

Alden B. Dow Home and Studio

Architect
Alden B. Dow

Year
1934–41

Location
315 Post Street
Midland
Michigan 48640
USA

abdow.org

The year after studying as an apprentice at Frank Lloyd Wright's Taliesin East, Alden B. Dow returned to his family home in Michigan. Here he built a combined house and studio for himself that was later described by *Architectural Digest* as 'one of the two most beautiful houses in the United States'. Being the son of the founder of the Dow Chemical Company, Dow repurposed cinder ash from the firm's furnaces to create modular masonry blocks he dubbed 'unit blocks'. These rhomboid-like forms offered greater stability than a standard cubic alternative. In the Alden B. Dow Home and Studio, he aligned them to form enclosing walls or staggered them to create open screens and landscaping elements. Intended as a low-cost construction system, the unit blocks form a central aesthetic of the house, which was built during the Great Depression and won Dow the grand prize for residential architecture at the 1937 Exposition Internationale des Arts et Techniques dans la Vie Moderne in Paris.

The family house and the architectural studio, sited on opposite sides of a central courtyard, are connected by Dow's personal studio. This timber-framed building, added in 1940, is topped with a copper roof, folded to create alternating windows and roof lights within its intricate structure. It overlooks a pond that was created by Dow by redirecting the stream that ran through his family's fruit orchards on the site, into which he built a conference room that appears to float half a metre below the waterline. The integration provided by the unit blocks between the studio and its surroundings embodies the architect's maxim that 'gardens never end and buildings never begin'. Internally the delineation between spaces is visually diminished, allowing glimpses between different areas set on split levels. A phosphorescent polymer ceiling — made by Dow Chemical — was added to the living room and glowed in the moonlight.

Guided tours are available with prior reservation.

🛏

Weaving House

Architect
Mark Hampton

Year
1957

Location
Woodbine Avenue
Lakeland
Florida 33803
USA

Available to rent via
various sites, including
plansmatter.com

Spanning the years 1941–66, the movement known as the
Sarasota School of Architecture was popularised by architects
such as Ralph Twitchell, Paul Rudolph, Victor Lundy, Gene Leedy
and Tim Seibert. These Sarasota Modern architects acted as an
East Coast complement to the Case Study House programme in
California of the same period; many of them had been inspired
by Frank Lloyd Wright's revolutionary Usonian style, used in his
designs for seminar buildings and faculty housing at the nearby
Florida Southern College. Wright's designs had introduced
a vocabulary of single-storey, flat-roof dwellings with deep
overhangs and clerestory windows. In the Florida climate, this
was employed by his acolytes to provide the necessary solar
shading and passive ventilation to the houses, made of lightweight
construction materials.

One of the architects, Mark Hampton, reinterpreted this
approach at the house he designed at Lake Hollingsworth (now
called the Weaving House after its current owner), which takes
a steel-framed grid structure as its starting point. Into this he
inserted a series of non-structural screens of walnut, textiles,
decorative glass, full-height sliding doors, timber brise-soleil
and a discreetly suspended fireplace to divide up the otherwise
open-plan space. To either end, concrete C-shaped structures
hold the house's utilitarian kitchen, storage space and utilities
and conceal two marble-lined bathrooms that look up to the sky.
External sliding panels of curtain wall glazing enable the living
space to open up between the internal terrazzo flooring and the
concrete terrace, into which the current owner — architectural
historian Andrew Weaving — later sunk a new pool designed in
collaboration with Hampton. The Weaving House not only retains
all its original features but its period furnishings have also been
carefully selected by Weaving, creating an authentic mid-century
home experience.

Aspen Meadows

Architect

Herbert Bayer

Year

1946–73

Location
845 Meadows Road
Aspen
Colorado 81611
USA

aspenmeadows.com

Over the course of three decades, with the assistance of Fritz Benedict, Herbert Bayer designed a collection of buildings across the Aspen Meadows campus. The Aspen Institute was the brainchild of industrialist Walter Paepcke, prompted by his wife, Elizabeth, who wanted to establish an international cultural and intellectual organisation in the former mining town of Aspen, Colorado. To help him achieve this, Paepcke approached Bayer, formerly the director of the newly founded printing and advertising workshop at the Bauhaus Dessau in Germany.

Bayer moved to the United States in the 1930s to design exhibitions at the Museum of Modern Art in New York. Although highly regarded as a photographer, typographer and graphic designer — skills that he put to use in marketing Aspen through its promotional posters — his initial training had been as an architectural apprentice in Austria and Germany.

The first building he completed was the Sundeck Restaurant (demolished in 1999), which sat on top of Aspen Mountain. This was followed seven years later by the hexagonal seminar building, which provided a base for the Aspen Music Festival, attracting prominent artists, musicians and thinkers. It is constructed from a prefabricated steel frame with breeze-block walls and decorated with a sgraffito mural of the surrounding mountains. Further facilities include the Institute of Humanistic Studies and the Walter Paepcke Memorial Building of 1962. Sculptures also created by Bayer are informally interspersed within the landscaping.

The three flat-roofed guest chalets, offering a total of 98 spacious suites, are constructed in lightweight, modular steel and prefabricated panels — familiar aspects of the Bauhaus style. The flank walls of the balconies are framed by a palette of bold yellow, red and blue, oriented to catch the sun, and provide a graphic identity for each chalet block.

CROWN
124 + 125
104 + 105

Watzek House

Architect

John Yeon

Year

1937

Location
1061 Southwest Skyline
Boulevard
Portland
Oregon 97221
USA

yeoncenter.uoregon.edu

Commissioned when the architect was only 26 years old, the Watzek House remains among John Yeon's most celebrated designs and is designated a National Historic Landmark. Yeon left university early following the death of his father, without gaining his architectural licence, and so when designing the Watzek House he completed the construction drawings under the auspices of the architectural practice A. E. Doyle, renowned for their bulky, Italianate designs. In contrast, the Watzek House is in the International Style, which Yeon infused with local materiality.

Approached from the road, the house appears rather blank and defensive, set on a rough-hewn stone base. There is a shift upon crossing the threshold of the house, from the wild nature of its surroundings into a pristine and refined oasis set around an open courtyard that appears deceptively contemporary despite its construction in 1937. The pared-down exterior is counterpointed by an immaculately detailed interior that draws strongly upon the exposed timber structures and tatami grids of traditional Japanese houses.

Many of Yeon's houses were built in timber, yet the material's use here is more pertinent given his client Aubrey Watzek's background as a lumber magnate. The architect stretched the expected proportions of the timber columns to give an impression of implausible lightness to the construction. He embraced the opportunities the grid offered: by liberating walls from their structural role he was able to slot different functions and materials within its structure, such as ventilation panels in the facade or marble for the fireplace, so that elements unite effortlessly, subservient to the grid's primary function of framing the views.

Since 2011 this early example of Pacific Northwest modernism has been open to the public, with regular informative tours organised by the Yeon Center.

Arcosanti

Architect
Paolo Soleri

Year
1970

Location
13555 South Cross L Road
Mayer
Arizona 86333
USA

arcosanti.org

In the middle of Arizona, 100 kilometres north of Phoenix, is an extraordinary utopian prototype city with futuristic concrete structures that wouldn't look out of place in a *Star Trek* film. Arcosanti was conceived by Italian-born architect Paolo Soleri, who based it on his concept of 'arcology'—the fusion of architecture and ecology. The architect first came to America in the late 1940s and worked under Frank Lloyd Wright at Taliesin West in Scottsdale, Arizona. When it came to urban planning, however, Soleri took a fundamentally different approach from Wright's Broadacre City concept, where the car reigned supreme. He instead took inspiration from the dense urban towns of his native country, believing that cities should be compact, built up and accessible on foot, thereby minimising the use of energy, raw materials and land; reducing waste and environmental pollution; and allowing human interaction with the natural environment.

In 1956 Soleri settled in Scottsdale and along with his wife made a lifelong commitment to the research of urban planning, setting up the Cosanti Foundation in 1964. Soleri wrote: 'The problem I am confronting is the present design of cities only a few stories high, stretching outward in unwieldy sprawl for miles. As a result, they literally transform the earth, turn farms into parking lots, wasting enormous amounts of time and energy transporting people, goods, and services over their expanses. My solution is urban implosion rather than explosion.'

Initially conceived as a much larger project, today Arcosanti is only 10 per cent complete and construction is still ongoing. The site is currently home to a range of buildings, including housing, an amphitheatre and a bell foundry, and in addition to an arts workshop programme hosts concerts and performances, drawing over 30,000 visitors a year. Overnight guests have the option of staying in modest guest rooms and dormitories or in one of three apartments with spectacular panoramic views of the desert.

Liljestrand House

Architect
Vladimir Ossipoff

Year
1952

Location
3300 Tantalus Drive
Honolulu
Hawaii 96822
USA

liljestrandhouse.org

Liljestrand House, designed by Vladimir Ossipoff, is built on a mountain site that was identified by the clients Betty and Howard Liljestrand when they were out hiking in 1946. The family house is largely open to the wind, rain and sun, with large, overhanging corrugated roofs and terraces (known as *lānai* in Hawaii) protecting it from almost everything bar the most severe weather. The building is characteristic of the Hawaiian Modern or *kama'aina* style that Ossipoff sought to establish in his commercial, civic and residential designs, to counteract the box-like housing constructed across the islands in the wake of the Second World War. Russian-born Ossipoff lived in Tokyo from the age of two until the Great Kantō Earthquake of 1923, which instilled in him a wariness of the potential force of nature. As a result, while training in California, Ossipoff developed a priority for climatic responsiveness out of respect for the land.

The lower level of the house, containing cellular spaces for the playroom, utility room, boys' bedroom and photography workshop, is protectively contained within a stone-faced concrete block retaining wall. The upper-level space, intended for the rest of the family, is visually more open. Constructed in a glazed timber-frame structure, it comprises the living and dining areas and further bedrooms. The house uses *shōji* sliding doors and timber louvres, exploiting the slope of the hill to create cross-ventilation through these spaces, which are sheltered on one side by the surrounding eucalyptus trees.

Exposed finishes throughout the house are dominated by the use of local monkeypod timber. The cabinetry and furniture, designed by the architect and built by Japanese craftsmen under the stewardship of Betty Liljestrand, remain as originally constructed. Today the house is managed by the Liljestrand Foundation, who offer guided tours on request.

🛏

Esherick
Mini-Mod

Architects
Joseph
Esherick

and
George
Homsey

Year
1967

Location
35255 Timber Ridge
Sea Ranch
California 95497
USA

esherickminimod.com

Sea Ranch is a unique community of homes sited on a 16-kilometre stretch of the Sonoma County coast, a two-and-a-half-hour drive north of San Francisco. It was conceived by Hawaii-based developer Oceanic Properties, who commissioned a team of architects to plan the site. They included the partners Moore, Lyndon, Turnbull and Whitaker, Joseph Esherick and landscape architect Lawrence Halprin. The development combined sustainable principles with modernist architecture, underpinned by a sense of environmental stewardship of the coastal landscape. As the town developed, Esherick, working with George Homsey, created a series of efficiently planned split-section cabins known as Mini-Mods, built as an experiment in economical construction for holiday homes that could be built anywhere across the site.

While the main community buildings were constructed on the exposed coastal site, the Mini-Mod cabins are nestled 1.5 kilometres away within the redwood forest. This recently restored and renovated cabin, by design collective Framestudio, comprising 64 square metres across three interconnected floors, is dominated by redwood and Douglas fir timber and features a kitchen-dining area overlooking the living space. Above is a queen-size bedroom with a bathroom, and a separate room with bunk-beds to one side. Each of these spaces has windows, creating visual connections with the surrounding forest along with the sound from the nearby ocean. With no neighbours in sight, the house also includes an external hot tub for four people.

The wider Sea Ranch community includes three recreation centres, including the Moonraker clubhouse, designed in an agricultural style with an interior dominated by vivid supergraphics by the landscape architect and graphic designer Barbara Stauffacher Solomon. In the Esherick Mini-Mod her enamelled artwork sits alongside works by American artists Robert Indiana and Alexander Girard.

Case Study House #26

Architect

Beverley David Thorne

Year

1962

Location
177 San Marino Drive
San Rafael
California 94901
USA

casestudyhouse.com

Case Study House #26 in San Rafael, California, close to San Francisco, was designed by Beverley David Thorne as an experiment to ascertain what construction method was most appropriate for developing a new neighbourhood in the steep, rocky landscape of Marin County. The building's steel frame was compared with one in timber and another in laminated wood, each accommodating a common brief for a four-bedroom, two-bathroom house within a 185-square-metre footprint. Thorne, who specialised in steel construction design, assisted with welding together the frame, which cantilevers over the hillside drop by 3 metres. The house is formed of eight 3-metre bays of exposed steel framing that delineate the living spaces internally and enable the introduction of sliding screens and movable wall panels, since these are non-loadbearing.

A single-storey, flat-roofed structure opens up to a second, mono-pitch roof that oversails the carport, creating a clerestory over the double-height living room. The flat roof also doubled as a heliport for a publicity stunt during the Case Study House tours in 1962 to demonstrate the stability of the steel frame. The house was initially named Harrison House after H. Harrison Fuller, an executive at Bethlehem Steel, the firm that had earlier provided the steel frame for Case Study House #22 (Stahl House, see page 88), but he died before its completion.

The exterior walls to the northwest face of the building are glazed, protected from the sun by two large overhanging roofs. The position of the house on the slope of a hill allowed it to be situated below the carport, affording a greater degree of privacy to the glazed living areas. Its current owners bought the house in 2015 and have sensitively restored it, furnishing it with period pieces. The entire home, accommodating up to six people, is available to rent for a minimum of two nights.

Schindler House

Architect
Rudolph M. Schindler

Year
1922

Location
833 North Kings Road
West Hollywood
California 90069
USA

makcenter.org

Since 1994 the MAK Center for Art and Architecture has been responsible for managing the Schindler House and the Mackey Apartments (see page 84), both designed by the Austrian-born architect Rudolph M. Schindler.

After seeing the Schindler House for the first time, in 1967, the renowned architecture critic and historian Reyner Banham described it in *Architectural Design* magazine as 'one of the most original and ingenious designs of the present century'. The single-storey house was designed by Schindler in 1922 — preceding the iconic houses of his European contemporaries — and it was highly influential in establishing the language of indoor-outdoor modernist living in California. The architect studied in Vienna and as an admirer of Frank Lloyd Wright was attracted by the prospect of working in America. In 1914 a job opportunity as a draughtsman took him to Chicago, and a few years later, after several attempts, he managed to persuade Wright to take him on at his office, where he worked on several notable projects. By 1921 Schindler had begun to think about starting a practice of his own, and a camping holiday in Yosemite with his wife Pauline that year was the catalyst and inspiration for him to build a studio-residence in West Hollywood.

Schindler joined forces with his friends Clyde and Marian Chase, and together they worked as architect and contractor, constructing a single building for both couples. Not only was the house a new kind of building, unlike anything else in America, but it also introduced a modern 'cooperative' way of living. Contrary to the convention of having separate living rooms, kitchens and so on, each adult had a 'studio', a series of zones that opened out via sliding doors to three intimate garden areas, each with an outdoor fireplace.

The construction of the home was especially experimental. The building sits on a concrete slab that was poured directly on

the ground and served as both the foundation and final floor finish. Additionally, the slab served as the surface for the on-site prefabrication of the walls, which were poured in a horizontal position and then lifted to create a solid back wall for each unit, linked by slots filled with either concrete or glazing. Schindler made use of honest and industrial materials such as smooth concrete, natural red-brown redwood, glass and canvas. Due not least to a lack of finances, the architect also designed much of the furniture himself.

The Chases moved out in 1924, which neatly coincided with Schindler's friend and collaborator Richard Neutra and his wife arriving in the US, and the couple soon moved in. In the 1930s the Schindlers separated and the home was divided, and in the following years the building saw further changes. Although Rudolph Schindler died in 1953, having designed over five hundred projects, Pauline Schindler remained in the house until her death in 1977. A year earlier, to preserve the building for the future, she established the non-profit organisation Friends of the Schindler House, who now own it.

Mackey Apartments

Architect
Rudolph M. Schindler

Year
1939

Location
1137 South Cochran Avenue
Los Angeles
California 90019
USA

makcenter.org

The Mackey Apartments in Los Angeles are today home to the artist residency programme of the MAK Center for Art and Architecture. In between residencies, however, the penthouse is available for overnight stays.

Seventeen years after designing his house in West Hollywood (see page 80), Rudolph M. Schindler transformed the traditional apartment block idiom found in the residential neighbourhoods of Los Angeles into his own spatial language: a compact apartment layout; interlocking 'space forms' on the facade; exceptional incorporation of natural light; built-in furniture; variable ceiling heights; and private outdoor gardens or mini-balconies. The ground-floor flats are mainly symmetrical, but the two-storey penthouse dramatically changes the spatial organisation of the upper floors, with a double-height living room, a dining mezzanine, two bedrooms and a separate study, all with marvellously framed views of the city.

Eames House

Architect

Charles and Ray Eames

Year

1949

Location
203 Chautauqua Boulevard
Pacific Palisades
Los Angeles
California 9027
USA

eamesfoundation.org

Designed by husband and wife Charles and Ray Eames in 1949 as their own home and studio, the Eames House was the eighth to be included in the Case Study House programme sponsored by *Arts and Architecture* magazine. Aside from their furniture designs, the Eames made over a hundred experimental films, often using a montage of materials 'as found'. They continued this approach in the design of their house. The building is expressed as a collage of industrial construction materials, such as steel doors, rubber paint, plastics and wire-mesh glass, alongside elements recognisably more domestic and complemented with strategically inserted colour, gold leaf and photographic panels.

The buildings were recessed into the sloping site to retain the existing meadow and eucalyptus trees, planted in the 1880s, and consist of two glass and steel rectangular boxes separated by a courtyard. One houses the studio and photography suite, the other the living quarters, with utility spaces for storage and bathrooms stacked to create double-height voids in the living and studio areas. With the doors of each block open, the courtyard becomes an external room, united within the 2.2-metre structural grid running across the site. This enabled the Eameses to appreciate the passing of seasons, and this was also emphasised through the landscaping, which was organised to respond to the changing temperature and humidity throughout the year. The home is filled with gifts from friends, family and colleagues and presented as it was at the time of Ray Eames's death in 1988.

Sharing the 5-acre site is a second house, designed by Charles Eames with Eero Saarinen. The single-storey building, known as Entenza House, uses similar framing and industrial materials to the Eames House and was built in 1950 as Case Study House #9. A variety of exterior and interior tours of the Eames House are available throughout the year, with proceeds supporting the conservation of this seminal building.

Stahl House

Architect
Pierre Koenig

Year
1960

Location
1635 Woods Drive
Los Angeles
California 90069
USA

stahlhouse.com

Immortalised by the photographer Julius Shulman as the iconic image of 1960s Los Angeles living, the Stahl House was number 22 in the series of Case Study Houses sponsored by *Arts and Architecture* magazine under its editor John Entenza between 1945 and 1966. The client, graphic designer Clarence 'Buck' Stahl, bought the site in 1954 and set about making it feasible to build upon, adding ivy and retaining walls of salvaged concrete rubble to create a secure base for the house. He appointed the architect Pierre Koenig in 1957, having admired his work published in the *Los Angeles Examiner* the previous year. It was Koenig's suggestion that the house should be part of the Case Study House programme — although construction delays meant that it nearly didn't meet the magazine's press deadline.

The single-storey building is set out in a simple flat-roofed, L-shape form around a swimming pool, with the private areas of the bedrooms, dressing room and bathroom nestled up against the hillside and wrapped in profiled steel decking panels to present a blank face on approach from the road. The construction made use of post-war industrial techniques such as arc welding, which reduced the need for bolts, rivets or cross-bracing. The framing was constructed in a single day by five men. For the wing containing the living areas, Koenig embraced the otherwise unbuildable site by dramatically cantilevering the steel frame by 3 metres over the hillside, its 6-metre plate-glass modules providing uninterrupted views of the city below. The roof has exposed steel beams and deep overhangs to prevent the house from overheating in the California sun. The fittings throughout this wing were designed to be subservient to the view: Koenig elevated the prefabricated fireplace chimney and high-level kitchen cupboards to create sight lines throughout the property. Afternoon or evening tours of this iconic house, which is still owned by the Stahl family, are available by prior reservation.

MHA Site Office

Architects

A. Quincy Jones

and

Whitney R. Smith

Year

1947

Location
Hanley Avenue
Brentwood
Los Angeles
California 90049
USA

mhasiteoffice.org

Initially conceived as a post-war commuter idyll for four musicians returning to California, the Mutual Housing Association (MHA) development plans expanded to accommodate five hundred families across an 800-acre site in Crestwood Hills, Los Angeles. Alongside the housing, the scheme incorporated cooperatively owned facilities, including a park, clubhouse, nursery school, amphitheatre, shop, health centre and petrol station, to help build the community socially and architecturally.

The pattern book of typologies created by architects A. Quincy Jones and Whitney R. Smith with structural engineer Edgardo Contini produced variations for 26 different single-storey, and occasionally split-level, homes. Their designs incorporated a palette of concrete blocks, large glazing, redwood siding and Douglas fir, enabling the MHA to make cost savings by using prefabricated fixtures and fittings and buying materials in bulk. However, the desire for standardisation was at odds with the complexity of the sloping site, and as a result of financial issues during construction only 85 dwellings were built, a majority of which were either destroyed in the Bel Air Fire of 1961 or have since been demolished.

Completed in 1947, the Site Office was the first structure of the development to be built and is cantilevered over a canyon on steel beams supported by a concrete pier. It is characteristic of many of the houses across the site, featuring a split roof of two mono-pitches supported on an expressed structural frame, and separated from the walls by clerestory glazing that runs around the perimeter of the house, creating uninterrupted views through the living spaces to the woodland beyond. It was converted to a house in 1952 and is now owned by Cory Buckner, an architect instrumental in the restoration of the remaining houses, and can be visited as part of a guided driving tour of the site.

Neutra VDL House and Studio

Architect

Richard Neutra

Year

1932/1965

Location
2300 Silver Lake Boulevard
Los Angeles
California 90039
USA

neutra-vdl.org

Between 1932 and 1970, Richard Neutra worked on dozens of architectural projects from his VDL House and Studio, situated in the hilly Los Angeles neighbourhood of Silver Lake. By the early 1930s he had established himself as one of the leading figures in Californian modernism but was yet to reap the financial rewards. After completing the Lovell Health House in 1929 he embarked on a tour of Europe, during which he met Cees van der Leeuw, owner of the Van Nelle Factory in Rotterdam and a champion of functionalist architecture. The philanthropic industrialist offered Neutra a low-interest loan to build himself a home where he could test his theories on space, materials, and the relationships between human well-being and the living environment.

Accepting the generous offer, in 1931 Neutra purchased a small plot overlooking Silver Lake Reservoir and set himself the task of designing a building that would house his family, his architecture practice and a bachelor's dwelling on a limited budget but without losing human comforts. The crisp white stucco building with ribbon windows is divided into two wings connected by a corridor, forming an H-shaped plan. A single-storey volume contained the studio apartment, whereas the two-storey volume comprised Neutra's office on the ground floor and the family dwelling on the upper floor. Neutra designed a series of courtyards and terraces sheltered by trees planted by the architect to create outdoor living spaces. A few years later, as the family grew, a further garden house was added. Tragically, in 1963 a fire destroyed much of the home, leaving only the garden house and the basement. Along with his son Dion, also an architect, Neutra used this opportunity to rebuild the house with up-to-date innovations and materials, and to add a penthouse.

Today the property is under the stewardship of Cal Poly Pomona university, which preserves and maintains it, offering weekly tours to visitors.

Grace Miller Guest House

Architect
Richard Neutra

Year
1937/2007

Location
2311 North Indian
Canyon Drive
Palm Springs
California 92262
USA

gracemillerhouse.com

By the 1930s the health benefits of fresh air and exercise had become widely recognised for improving the overall standard of living. In 1929, shortly after arriving in the US, Austrian-born Richard Neutra was commissioned to design the Lovell Health House in Los Angeles, now widely regarded as one of his masterpieces. The house boasts an open-air fitness suite, rooms for sunbathing and sleeping out in the open, and various dietary and therapeutic services, all designed to support the mental and bodily health of Dr Lovell and his family. Neutra's interest in therapeutic architecture continued, and when he was approached in 1936 by Grace Lewis Miller, an instructor in the Mensendieck System of Functional Exercises, to design a light-filled house that would also incorporate an exercise studio, he could not refuse.

Despite it being a small commission, the house marks an important beginning in Neutra's Palm Springs desert house projects—his best-known being the Kaufmann House of 1946. Miller, accompanied by her architect, chose a 2.5-acre site on Indian Avenue (now Indian Canyon Drive) in the open desert, five minutes' drive from the Palm Springs village centre. Over the following months they exchanged dozens of letters and detailed plans. The house was completed in 1937, and in March that year Miller wrote to Neutra asking him to work on an additional building: 'I am planning to build something to house my two boys next season … some kind of guest house.' A year later Neutra completed the designs, but owing to financial constraints it was never built.

In 2000, after years of neglect, the Miller house went up for sale. Its new owner began a lengthy restoration process that included the realisation of the Guest House in 2007, based upon Neutra's original plans. The Guest House, which accommodates two people, can be rented out for a two-night minimum stay.

The Wexler

Architects

Donald Wexler

and

Richard Harrison

Year

1960

Location
El Rancho Vista Estate
Vía Roberto Miguel
Palm Springs
California 92262
USA

acmehouseco.com

Located northeast of Palm Springs International Airport, the El Rancho Vista Estate was the first group of houses developed by Donald Wexler, a leading figure in desert modernism, and his partner Richard Harrison. When creating this series of new homes, Wexler's key revelation was how inappropriate the use of timber was for the locality, since its scarcity necessitated huge costs for shipping materials to site. In contrast, lightweight steel frames — typically used in the construction of schools — could be fabricated in factories in Los Angeles and transported to site, taking only five trucks to haul enough components for three houses. The frame was then aligned to a template, set out on the concrete slab and bolted into place, enabling the assembly of the main structure in around four hours. After this initial construction, an entire home could be completed in about a month.

This partially prefabricated approach enabled the creation of a lighter aesthetic embracing modernism's industrialisation, building upon the Miesian frame structures Wexler developed while working for architects Richard Neutra and William F. Cody. Within the steel frame, Wexler created a palette of 2.4-metre modular panels of steel, timber louvres, breeze-block or stone to provide individuality to the properties. Further variations on the modular type were created through the addition of distinctive cantilevered and zig-zag roof forms, akin to the Googie architecture that defines Los Angeles and Palm Springs. The rising cost of steel, however, scuppered plans for mass construction.

Approximately 75 houses were built, with several now available as holiday homes, including this recently renovated three-bedroom house furnished with mid-century furniture. Its bedrooms are separated from an open-plan living-dining-kitchen area, with large floor-to-ceiling sliding glass screens that open up to the private walled garden and a sunken swimming pool.

Georgia O'Keeffe Home and Studio

Architect

Maria Chabot

Year

1949

Location
12 Palvadera Road
Abiquiú
New Mexico 87510
USA

okeeffemuseum.org

In 1945, American artist Georgia O'Keeffe bought a ruined nineteenth-century Spanish Colonial-style house in Abiquiú, 100 kilometres northwest of Santa Fe, from the Catholic Church. She set about restoring and reconfiguring it with the help of her friend Maria Chabot. Having underpinned the foundations, Chabot rebuilt the walls with clay from the village cemetery; however, finding the necessity to re-mud the exterior walls each year arduous, O'Keeffe later covered these in stucco. Plate-glass windows were cut into the traditional thick adobe walls, often taking up the full width of the room, and supplemented by skylights to further illuminate what would traditionally have been dark interiors. A wide window inserted into the corner affords views out across the surrounding New Mexico desert. The sole curve to the plan holds a modernist guest bathroom, replacing the only room of the house O'Keeffe and Chabot were unable to save. Chabot also replaced the traditional mud flooring with cement and cork and installed modern plumbing, radiant panel heaters and fluorescent lighting.

The house is divided into four quadrants to contain different functions: utility spaces and a double garage to the north, guest bedrooms and bathroom to the east, a library and art store to the south, and living and dining spaces to the west. O'Keeffe's studio, bedroom and bathroom are located in a separate restored outbuilding. The courtyard layout allowed O'Keeffe to make the most of the desert sunlight and expansive skies. The garden was built with an irrigation system, enabling plants not indigenous to the area to thrive.

The building and surrounding views were a huge source of inspiration for the artist, and she produced no fewer than twenty paintings and drawings of the patio and its black door. The home and studio, which are in the main how O'Keeffe left them in 1984, are open to the public for seasonal tours with advance booking.

Latin America

Museo Casa Estudio Diego Rivera y Frida Kahlo

Architect

Juan O'Gorman

Year

1931

Location
Avenida Altavista
& Diego Rivera
San Ángel Inn
Álvaro Obregón
Mexico City 01060
Mexico

estudiodiegorivera.inba.
gob.mx

The buildings designed by Mexican architect Juan O'Gorman between 1928 and 1937 are considered to be the first functionalist constructions in Mexico. Although heavily influenced by Le Corbusier (O'Gorman reportedly read *Vers une architecture* four times at the age of nineteen), his architecture of cubic volumes featured rendered walls painted in deep blues, reds, yellows and browns, contrary to the European trend of stark white. After completing the Cecil Crawford O'Gorman house he designed for his father in 1931, the architect was commissioned to design a pair of houses for his friends the artists Diego Rivera and Frida Kahlo on the adjacent plot. The couple lived separately in two independent structures that were connected by an elevated bridge. The buildings are situated in the San Ángel neighbourhood, a district in southern Mexico City renowned for its colonial-era architecture, cobbled streets and bougainvillea-covered houses.

Rivera, a mural painter and at the time the better-known of the two, lived in the larger of the two buildings. It incorporates a generous double-height studio where he painted more than 3,000 works. The facades of both buildings are painted in bold block colours — Rivera's in white and reddish-brown; Kahlo's in a vivid blue — and feature industrial elements such as an external spiral staircase, sawtooth roof and exposed electrical conduits.

Kahlo lived in her house until the couple's divorce in 1939, and Rivera continued to work in his until his death in 1957, after which his daughter inherited it and made several dramatic changes, including the removal of the connecting bridge. In 1997 the Instituto Nacional de Bellas Artes returned the structures to their original 1930s floor plans and converted them into a museum dedicated to both artists. Rivera's is filled with his paintings, papier-mâché works and eclectic objects, whereas Kahlo's features temporary exhibitions.

Casa Luis Barragán

Architect
Luis Barragán

Year
1948

Location
12–14 General Francisco Ramírez
Ampliación Daniel Garza, Miguel Hidalgo
Mexico City 11840
Mexico

casaluisbarragan.org

'My house is my refuge, an emotional piece of architecture, not a cold piece of convenience', said the Mexican architect Luis Barragán, who lived in the home he designed for himself until his death in 1988. Best known for his saturated 'Mexican colours' and play on light, contrasting shadows and vertical and horizontal planes, Barragán moved to Mexico City in the mid-1930s and embarked on an intense period of work fusing international modernism with the local vernacular. A decade later, Barragán became jaded by the constraints imposed by his clients and began a career in real estate development. He acquired land in a working-class area of Tacubaya, where he designed private gardens as well as his first house, Casa Ortega. A few years later he sold that house to build Casa Luis Barragán on the same street.

Externally, Casa Luis Barragán is unassuming, a blank facade blending in with its neighbours that promises much more on the inside. The building is divided across two levels, and throughout one moves from small, dimly lit, low-ceilinged corridors to large, dramatic double-height spaces, and back again. The rooms are serene, with a dreamlike quality and a hint of surrealism, such as in the iconic cantilevered floating stairs. Materials are left in their natural state, for example in the roughly plastered walls and volcanic rock tiles. The back of the house opens up to a garden, with a two-storey window with cross-like mullions—Barragán was an observant Catholic, and discreet crosses appear throughout the house. At the top of the building is a rooftop with high walls, obscuring the street below—visitors are encouraged to focus on the bright orange and pink of the walls, which frame the blue sky.

Since Barragán's death this highly personalised building, which retains all of the architect's furniture, objects, collection of artworks and library, has been run as a museum. Managed by the Fundación de Arquitectura Tapatía Luis Barragán, it is a mecca for architects and design aficionados from around the world.

Casa sobre el Arroyo

Architect

Amancio Williams

Year

1943–45

Location
3998 Quintana
Mar del Plata
Buenos Aires B7602
Argentina

facebook.com/
museocasasobreelarroyo

Despite years of neglect, vandalism and even an arson attack in 2004, one of the great masterpieces of modernism in Latin America can be still visited by the public. Casa sobre el Arroyo (House over the Brook), situated in the popular resort city of Mar del Plata, was designed by Amancio Williams for his father, Alberto Williams, a noted musician. Amancio Williams was a prominent figure in the modern movement in Argentina and began work on Casa sobre el Arroyo a few years after graduating from the University of Buenos Aires, in collaboration with his wife, Delfina Gálvez Bunge de Williams. The distinctive house with its bridge-like reinforced concrete structure appears to hover weightlessly above a stream. It was built on the wooded outskirts of the seaside city, on a beautiful 5-acre plot of land that was divided by a stream and only accessible on one side. Williams described the house as 'a form in space that does not deny nature'. Such care and attention was given to the construction that the concrete was extensively laboratory-tested to ensure the quality was sufficient to offer both the structural and surface characteristics desired.

Entrance to the house is via dimly lit staircases placed at either end of the building. Climbing to the top of the stairs, visitors are hit with light and the expanse of space of the main level. On one side of the house there is a large open-plan room for the living, dining and sitting areas, which would originally have been separated only by the furniture, also designed by Williams. The bedrooms were placed on the other side of the building, with windows that wrap around the entire structure. The fire devastated most of the interior, including the wood panelling; however, at the time of writing there are plans to restore the building to its original state.

Casa Curutchet

Architect

Le Corbusier

Year

1948–53

Location
320 Avenida 53
La Plata
Buenos Aires B1900
Argentina

capbacs.com

In 1929 Le Corbusier made his first trip to Argentina. Of his arrival, he recalled: 'All of a sudden, I saw Buenos Aires. This image stayed with me, intense.' Nineteen years later, Dr Pedro Domingo Curutchet, a progressive surgeon, contacted Le Corbusier in Paris asking him to design a small house and clinic in La Plata, a city a few miles south of Buenos Aires. Keen to realise a project in South America, and despite being busy with the Cité Radieuse in Marseille, Le Corbusier accepted the commission and enlisted Argentine architect Amancio Williams to oversee the construction.

The Maison Curutchet was built on an irregular, narrow site between existing buildings and opposite a small park. It is formed of two volumes, one at the front facing the street, which housed the clinic, and a square volume at the rear intended as the family dwelling. A spectacular poplar tree separates the two volumes and rises through all four storeys. The building, with its fully glazed facade and concrete brise-soleil, is raised on pilotis, allowing for a garage on the ground floor. A dramatic external ramp takes you through an 'architectural promenade' to the first floor, while on the second floor Le Corbusier placed the social spaces: an open-plan double-height living room and dining room, a large terrace with views towards the park, and the kitchen. At the top of the house are the bedrooms.

Unfortunately, the project was dogged by complications. Williams left the project, and Simón Ungar took over, making considerable changes on site without Curutchet's approval. By the time the house was completed in 1953 the family's needs had changed, and they lived in it for only a short time. In the following years Curutchet used it sporadically, and it began to deteriorate. In 1986 the building underwent restoration and it is now a National Historic Monument, leased to the College of Architects of the Province of Buenos Aires. The house is open to the public for self-guided tours.

🛏

Hotel Antumalal

Architect
Jorge Elton

Year
1950

Location
Camino Pucón a
Villarrica Km. 2
Pucón 4920000
Chile

antumalal.com

Hotel Antumalal was the brainchild of Czech-born Guillermo Pollak, his wife Catalina and her mother, Davit. In the 1940s they dreamt of building a hotel on a beautiful site 2 kilometres from the city of Pucón in Chile's northern Lake District, where they already ran a popular tea room. Guillermo approached the Chilean president, Gabriel González Videla, with a request for a loan to build a work of architecture that would make Chile proud. Keen to promote tourism, he helped to secure them a loan and the Pollaks set to work, commissioning the Chilean architect Jorge Elton, a graduate of the Universidad Católica in Santiago, to design a sixteen-room hotel.

Perched on top of a cliff and surrounded by 12 acres of private gardens, this striking building appears to hover dramatically over the lake when viewed from afar. Elton carefully integrated the hotel within the natural landscape, retaining all of the existing trees. It comprises two wings, forming an L-shape. The single-storey wing contains the guest rooms, and the two-storey wing includes the common areas (the bar, living room and dining room, with a suspended terrace), with further guest rooms, including two-family suites, on the upper floor. The volumes of concrete, glass and stone are supported on chunky pilotis with vertical planes painted in red and horizontal planes in white. The ceiling slabs of the guest rooms extend beyond the building, creating prominent eaves and blurring the boundary between outdoor and indoor, a sense further accentuated by the large areas of glazing, giving panoramic views. Internally the rooms are equipped with furniture designed by Elton and are complete with log-burning fireplaces, walls veneered in wood, floors in leather and sheepskin rugs.

Since its opening in 1950 the hotel has been sympathetically updated, including the addition of a swimming pool carved into the rock in the 1960s and additional secluded chalets.

Casa
de Vidro

Architect
Lina Bo Bardi

Year
1950–51

Location
200 Rua General Almério
de Moura
Morumbi
São Paulo 05690-080
Brazil

institutobardi.com.br

Surrounded by dense rainforest, the Casa de Vidro (Glass House) appears to float dramatically above one's head. The house was the first built project by Italian-born architect Lina Bo Bardi, who along with her husband, the curator and art dealer Pietro Maria Bardi, emigrated to Brazil in 1946, where they immersed themselves in the local culture. It is situated in the Morumbi district on the outskirts of São Paulo, on a site that had been deforested and was initially earmarked by São Paulo Museum of Art for a studio building to host visiting artists. When those plans fell through the Bardis decided to build themselves a home there instead, with a view that it would also act as a meeting point for artists: over the years its visitors included Max Bill, Gio Ponti, Alexander Calder and John Cage.

Bo Bardi took full advantage of the steeply sloping terrain and elevated the building on slim steel columns, placing the social spaces at the front and the private areas, such as the bedrooms and staff quarters, at the back. The rear of the building sits at ground level at the top of the slope. The entrance is located at the centre of the house, where an elegant steel staircase invites you to ascend into a spacious open-plan living area. Surrounded by floor-to-ceiling windows, the place is reminiscent of a tree-house, a sense further emphasised by the tree growing through the building within an interior glazed courtyard. Bo Bardi carefully designed each minute detail of the interior, from the door handles and lighting to the chairs. She also transformed the surrounding land into a tropical forest by replanting native vegetation.

The couple lived here for forty years and as avid collectors filled their home with an eclectic mix of objects. Today this seminal building, which remains virtually unaltered, serves as the headquarters of the Instituto Lina Bo e P. M. Bardi and can be visited by the public with prior booking.

Casa Modernista

Architect
Gregori Warchavchik

Year
1927–28

Location
325 Rua Santa Cruz
Vila Mariana
São Paulo 04121-000
Brazil

museudacidade.prefeitura.
sp.gov.br

The Ukrainian architect Gregori Warchavchik arrived in São Paulo in 1923, a year after its pivotal 1922 Modern Art Week, a festival where for seven days Brazilian artists created some of the most avant-garde works ever seen, firmly establishing the country's modernist movement. Although modernist architecture was already established in Europe and even in parts of South America, such as Argentina and Uruguay, Warchavchik was largely responsible for championing the aesthetic in Brazil. He opened his architecture practice in São Paulo in 1925, and his own house, designed a couple of years later on Rua Santa Cruz, is considered the first modernist building in the country.

When completed, the house, with its stark symmetrical facade and devoid of superfluous decoration, attracted a great deal of attention. The building was constructed on a large plot of land and is surrounded by sculptural planting in a tropical garden designed by Warchavchik's wife, Mina Klabin, the daughter of an affluent São Paulo industrialist family. Klabin became a pioneer in modern Brazilian landscaping, using native plants to complement and give leverage to Brazilian modern movement architecture. Following Le Corbusier's visit to Casa Modernista in 1929, Warchavchik became Brazil's CIAM (International Congresses of Modern Architecture) representative.

As his family grew, Warchavchik made some slight adaptations to the building, and they lived there until the 1970s. During the years that followed, however, it stood unoccupied and in a state of deterioration and uncertainty; Warchavchik's work occupied a delicate position in the history of Brazilian modernist architecture, sometimes regarded as not being authentically modernist enough, or criticised for being too European. Following a 2008 restoration by the city of São Paulo, however, the building opened as a house museum, and the public can now explore and appreciate this critical contribution to Brazilian architecture.

Casa Oscar Americano

Architect
Oswaldo Arthur Bratke

Year
1953

Location
Fundação Maria Luiza e
Oscar Americano
4077 Avenida Morumbi
Morumbi
São Paulo 05607-200
Brazil

fundacaooscaramericano.
org.br

Casa Oscar Americano is located in Morumbi, a district located over the Pinheiros River valley and approximately 15 kilometres from São Paulo's downtown. The area began to be developed in the mid-1940s and soon became one of the most affluent neighbourhoods of São Paulo. Oswaldo Arthur Bratke, a leading figure in Brazilian modernist architecture, devised the urban plan for the area, inspired by garden neighbourhoods. In 1950 the engineer and entrepreneur Oscar Americano, a friend of Bratke's, commissioned him to design a large family house on a substantial plot with lush vegetation consisting mainly of pine and eucalyptus.

Bratke placed the house at the top of a sloping site, surrounded by the natural landscape. With its low horizontal volume, light facade, ample glazing and strong relationship to the outdoors, the house is reminiscent of the work of Richard Neutra or Mies van der Rohe. The main living areas, bedrooms, bathrooms, dining room, office, kitchen and maid's room occupy the raised ground floor, while the service areas and garage are tucked below, making use of the sloping terrain. A large internal courtyard is at the centre of the building, further enhancing the dialogue with the surrounding landscape.

The magnificent garden, expanding to 75,000 square metres, was masterfully designed by Brazilian landscape architect Otávio Augusto Teixeira Mendes, who reinstated some of the native Atlantic Forest trees to the land. He planted more than 20,000 seedlings to create expressive tree groupings contrasting in size, colour and texture.

The family lived in the house for twenty years. In 1974, following the death of his wife, Oscar Americano donated it and its contents to the city of São Paulo. In 1980 it opened to the public, displaying the family's extensive art collection, including sixteenth-century paintings and furniture, in a museum-like layout.

Casa Walther Moreira Salles

Architect
Olavo Redig de Campos

Year
1948–52

Location
476 Rua Marquês
de São Vicente
Gávea
Rio de Janeiro 22451-040
Brazil

ims.com.br

The current headquarters of the Instituto Moreira Salles, a cultural centre promoting photography, literature, art and music, was the former home of Walther Moreira Salles, a wealthy banker and Brazilian ambassador to Washington. Salles had two main passions: banking and the arts. In the late 1940s he commissioned the Brazilian architect Olavo Redig de Campos to design him a large house in Gávea, a neighbourhood south of Rio de Janeiro, on a generous site encompassing 10,000 square metres and surrounded by the lush Tijuca Forest. Rio was emerging from its colonial past to become a modern metropolis, and Brazilian architects such as Campos developed a style that combined international modernism with a Brazilian vernacular. In the Moreira Salles house the architect drew inspiration from traditional Carioca farmhouses.

The building was planned around an internal courtyard, with a large social wing used for frequent receptions, parties and political ceremonies, served by a partially hidden service area. The entire social wing, with its vast areas of glazing, looks out to the central court with a garden and pool beyond and magnificent views of the mountains. At the opposite side of the court there is a smaller, private wing protected by functional and decorative brise-soleil. The abstract garden, along with a striking ceramic fresco, was designed by the painter and landscape designer Roberto Burle Marx. Luxurious materials and striking patterns feature throughout, including the red and white Italian marble floor in a bold geometric design. Campos highly personalised the design of the house for his client, with the door handles, for example, cast to fit Moreira Salles's hands. The family lived in the house until 1980, and in 1999 it was restored and converted into a modern gallery showcasing temporary exhibitions as well as Moreira Salles's art collection. It is open to the public with free admission.

Chácara do Céu

Architect

Wladimir Alves de Souza

Year

1956

Location
93 Rua Murtinho Nobre
Santa Teresa
Rio de Janeiro 20241-050
Brazil

museuscastromaya.com.br

Wladimir Alves de Souza, an architect, restorer and professor of architectural theory at the Universidade Federal do Rio de Janeiro, experimented with a variety of styles, ranging from eclectic to neoclassical. One of his best-known buildings is the Chácara do Céu in Rio de Janeiro, a modernist residence built for the wealthy industrialist and art patron Raymundo Ottoni de Castro Maya. The businessman inherited an old house dating from 1876 in the Santa Teresa neighbourhood, which he demolished in 1954. He commissioned his friend Souza to design a new modern home on the site, while the garden, with magnificent views of the city of Rio, was designed by the Brazilian landscape architect Roberto Burle Marx.

Castro Maya's home has now been converted into a museum and today houses his vast art collection as well as hosting temporary exhibitions. Two rooms have been preserved with their original furniture and decor in order to retain the character of the house. The adjoining Parque das Ruínas, with spectacular views from the top floor of its once abandoned colonial mansion, is worth a visit.

Chez Georges

Architect
Wladimir Alves de Souza

Year
1974

Location
90 Ladeira do Meireles
Santa Teresa
Rio de Janeiro 20241-340
Brazil

georges.life

The now named Chez Georges, originally completed in 1974, is one of several residential projects Wladimir Alves de Souza worked on in the Santa Teresa neighbourhoods of Rio. The villa, which Souza expertly integrated into the landscape, uses contrasting materials including raw concrete, tile and timber. Perched high on a hill, the house is surrounded by lush vegetation. The patio with striking tall concrete pergola and a 6-metre wooden door are among the villa's structural standout features, as are the soaring vaulted concrete ceilings.

In 2019 two entrepreneurs, Pierre Bident Moldeva and Olivier Verwilghen, converted the villa into a stylish hotel. It now offers seven private suites that can be rented out either separately or in their entirety, accommodating up to fourteen people. The suites range from 25 to 49 square metres, many with floor-to-ceiling windows overlooking Santa Teresa. Additionally the villa boasts a separate music studio. Although not original, the interior furnishings take inspiration from the period, with mid-century modern pieces. Guests can also enjoy a 14-metre pool and a rooftop panoramic viewing area with a 360-degree view of Guanabara Bay and Sugarloaf Mountain.

Europe

Maison
La Roche

Architects
Le Corbusier

and
Pierre
Jeanneret

Year
1923–25

Location
8–10 Square du Docteur-
Blanche
Paris 75016
France

fondationlecorbusier.fr

Maison La Roche marks a significant point in Le Corbusier's period of experimental 'white villas'. Along with his cousin Pierre Jeanneret, with whom he collaborated for about twenty years, here Le Corbusier explored many of the architectural theories he later put into practice. The building is located in the 16th arrondissement of Paris (a twenty-minute walk from the Le Corbusier apartment; see page 120) on a plot of land that was formerly the gardens of the surrounding houses. The villa, which was completed in 1925, is approached by a private road and is surrounded by trees, but with urban houses in close proximity.

The L-shaped building was conceived as two homes, one for Le Corbusier's friend Raoul La Roche, a wealthy Swiss banker, and the other for his brother, Albert Jeanneret. Le Corbusier explained: 'One accommodates a family with children, and is thus composed of a quantity of small rooms and all amenities needed by a family, whereas the second is designed for a bachelor, owner of a collection of modern paintings, and passionate about art.' The two private residential parts of the building are adjacent to each other and form the long part of the 'L', while a 'public' curved gallery space raised on pilotis sits at a right angle, separated by a large hallway. Le Corbusier used staircases, sweeping curved ramps, a linking bridge in the dramatic triple-height space, and a band of windows which cast light and shadows throughout the interior, to encourage visitors to take an 'architectural promenade' through the building. The use of colour at Maison La Roche involved a carefully considered palette of seventeen muted shades.

After its completion the building suffered a series of technical problems, but La Roche remained an accommodating and generous client. The house has undergone several restoration campaigns and in 1996 was classified as a historical monument. It is open to the public, managed by the Fondation Le Corbusier, which is based next door in the Maison Jeanneret.

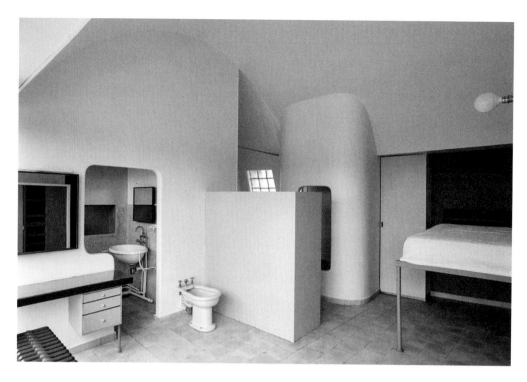

Studio-Apartment
Le Corbusier

Architects
Le Corbusier

and

Pierre Jeanneret

Year
1931–34

Location
Immeuble Molitor
24 Rue Nungesser et Coli
Paris 75016
France

fondationlecorbusier.fr

Le Corbusier regarded the elements of urbanism to be the sky, trees, steel and concrete—and in that order. These ideas would manifest in the Immeuble Molitor apartments, where he lived with his wife, dog (named Pinceau, meaning 'paintbrush') and housekeeper from the age of 46 until his death in 1965, aged 77.

The Immeuble Molitor, built between 1931 and 1934, was commissioned by private real estate developers, who instructed Le Corbusier and Pierre Jeanneret not only to design the apartment block but also to find potential buyers. The seven-storey building is located on the outskirts of Paris, and it was the first in the world to have an entire glass facade at front and back, which allowed maximum light to enter it. The reinforced frame structure created a 'free plan', with two or three apartments on each floor fitted only with a bathroom, giving the owners flexibility and choice in deciding how to partition the rooms themselves. Luxuries such as lifts, central heating, a laundry room, cellar and garages were incorporated to create a truly modern building.

It was typical in Paris for servants to be housed in the eaves of buildings; here, however, Le Corbusier placed the staff quarters on the ground floor and negotiated with the developer to take the top two storeys and roof terrace for himself. He converted them at his own expense into an apartment and studio—a brick-faced double-height room full of daylight for painting and writing. Both have recently undergone significant restoration by the Fondation Le Corbusier and are now open to the public. Replicas of the furniture, much of it unique—such as the unusually high bed, which allowed for views of Boulogne over the balcony—have been installed to match how the apartment stood towards the end of Le Corbusier's life.

Pavillon Suisse

Architect
Le Corbusier

and

Pierre Jeanneret

Year
1933

Location
Cité Internationale
Universitaire de Paris
7K Boulevard Jourdan
Paris 75014
France

fondationsuisse.fr

Commissioned by the Swiss government, the Pavillon Suisse is one of the 37 student residence buildings of the Cité Internationale Universitaire in Paris. Professor Rudolf Fueter, a mathematician and dean of the University of Zurich, commissioned Le Corbusier to design the building. Although initially reluctant, having lost the 1927 competition for the Palace of the League of Nations in Geneva, Le Corbusier accepted the project, collaborating on it with his cousin Pierre Jeanneret.

Pavillon Suisse was completed in 1933 on a tight budget and acted as a testing ground for Le Corbusier's vision of collective housing. Many of the ideas expressed here are evident in his later work: pilotis, roof gardens, the free design of the facade, horizontal windows and a free ground plan. The main building, which houses the bedrooms, is a reinforced concrete block with a lightweight steel frame raised on sculptural concrete pilotis, positioned close to the centre of the building to give the impression that the structure is floating. The south side of the building is completely covered in glazing, whereas in contrast the north is a composition of concrete blocks and small square windows. Connecting buildings are used as circulation areas and include a single-storey entrance lobby and lounge-refectory. The accommodation was designed to house 42 students, with each bedroom almost identical, measuring 2.8 by 6 metres with south-facing windows. Jean Prouvé was responsible for the bedroom furniture and interior planning.

In 1940 the building was occupied by the Nazis, and some of the original features, such as the photographic wall in the lounge, were destroyed (replaced in 1948 with a painted mural by Le Corbusier). More recently, the building has gone through extensive renovation and restoration. Stays of a minimum of two weeks are available during the summer months to students, researchers, architects and others with an interest in Le Corbusier.

Maison du Brésil

Architect
Le Corbusier

Year
1953–59

Location
Cité Internationale
Universitaire de Paris
7L Boulevard Jourdan
Paris 75014
France

maisondubresil.org

In 1953 Le Corbusier was invited by Brazilian architect Lúcio Costa to work with him on a project similar to his Pavillon Suisse, this time for accommodation for Brazilian students. Commissioned by the Brazilian government under President Juscelino Kubitschek, the building at Cité Internationale Universitaire de Paris was also intended to promote relations between France and Brazil. Initial designs had already been drafted by Costa before Le Corbusier became involved. Subsequently, Le Corbusier made a significant number of modifications, and eventually Costa decided to remove his name from the project. The building was inaugurated in 1959.

Maison du Brésil shares certain similarities with the earlier project: a large rectangular volume raised on pilotis houses the bedrooms, with smaller masses linked to it. Visually, however, with its use of intense colours and brise-soleil, it bears a closer relationship to the architect's Unité d'habitation buildings (see page 142). Charlotte Perriand and Jean Prouvé were responsible for the design of the furniture in the bedrooms, which all face west. Additional facilities were placed in two single-storey wings east and west of the main building, joined underneath the main block by a curved passageway with expanses of glass.

Le Corbusier placed the director's apartment, administrative rooms and a library in the west wing; and the communal spaces, such as a lounge and a theatre, in the east wing.

Over the years Maison du Brésil became run down, and in 1997 it closed for renovation. The works were carried out in accordance with the Fondation Le Corbusier, and the building reopened its doors in 2000. During the summer months, single and double rooms can be rented for a minimum of three nights.

Van Doesburg House

Architect
Theo van Doesburg

Year
1926–30

Location
29 Rue Charles Infroit
Meudon 92190
France

vandoesburghuis.com

In 1917 the Dutch artist, theorist and writer Theo van Doesburg, along with Piet Mondrian, founded the De Stijl movement and magazine of the same name. His house, situated in Meudon, a southwestern suburb of Paris, is the manifestation of his views on art and life in an architectural form. In 1921 Van Doesburg moved to Weimar in Germany with his wife, Nelly van Doesburg, an avant-garde musician, hoping to secure a teaching post at the Bauhaus. Here he became increasingly interested in architecture and met the young Dutch architect Cornelis van Eesteren. The two collaborated on a series of architectural models and exhibited them in 1923 in the first De Stijl exhibition in Paris.

Following an inheritance from Nelly's father, the couple bought a strip of land to build a studio-house for themselves in France, where Van Doesburg was able to put his ideas into practice. The design began in 1926, and it took four years to complete the construction. The building comprises two interlocking cubes that are vertically staggered to create two additional facades. One of the cubes, with windows several metres high, was intended for Van Doesburg's studio, while the other contains the living accommodation. He used colour sparingly but boldly—external doors are painted red, yellow and blue in an otherwise wholly white rendered facade. The muted interior walls in shades of grey are accented with coloured tiled floors and a stained-glass skylight in the library.

In March 1931, only a few months after they had moved in, Van Doesburg died of a heart attack. Nelly remained in the house for the rest of her life, promoting her husband's work and fulfilling his wishes for the house to become a mecca for people in the arts. In the 1980s it was donated to the Dutch state, and the Van Doesburg House Foundation was formed. The house hosts an artist residency programme and opens to the public once a week with prior booking.

Villa Savoye

Architects

Le Corbusier

and

Pierre Jeanneret

Year

1929–31

Location
82 Rue de Villiers
Poissy 78300
France

villa-savoye.fr

Located in Poissy, a suburb 25 kilometres west of Paris, the Villa Savoye is perhaps Le Corbusier's best-known building and the first to become listed as a French historical monument. It was built between 1929 and 1931 for wealthy clients Pierre and Eugénie Savoye as a weekend and summer retreat.

All of Le Corbusier's Five Points of a New Architecture are clearly expressed in the Villa Savoye. The villa sits in the middle of a large green lawn and appears to float in space. On the ground floor are rooms for the staff and a garage; the bulk of the house is on the first floor, in a rectangular box elevated on a grid of pilotis and with a strip of windows wrapping around it. A curved glass facade on the ground floor screens the entrance; once inside, you are presented with two options: to climb the sculptural spiral staircase to the first floor, or walk up the ceremonial ramp that continues to the rooftop.

The plan of the house is relatively straightforward, with the bedrooms, guest room, kitchen, bathroom and living room arranged in an L-shape around a terrace. A huge floor-to-ceiling glass wall in the living room opens up to the terrace. The kitchen, where Eugénie Savoye spent much of her time, is functional and industrial with white ceramic-tiled worktops and aluminium-fronted built-in cupboards. The bathroom is particularly unusual for its square sunken bath and concrete lounge 'chair' covered in blue mosaic.

Despite being widely regarded as his masterpiece, the villa's innovative design and construction led to several problems, such as a leaking roof and windows. The Savoyes eventually abandoned the building in 1940, and it began to deteriorate further. A public petition saved it from demolition, and it was taken over by the French state in 1958. In 1997 the building was fully restored and, although mainly unfurnished, it opened its doors to the public. Visitors are free to tour the house unaccompanied.

Maison
Louis Carré

Architect
Alvar Aalto

Year
1956–59

Location
2 Chemin du
Saint-Sacrement
Bazoches-sur-Guyonne
78490
France

maisonlouiscarre.fr

Once private and only open to the public on rare occasions, the Maison Louis Carré is now managed by the Association Alvar Aalto en France and can be visited every weekend aside from in the winter months. It was commissioned by the well-known art dealer Louis Carré, who in the 1950s bought a large plot of land near Bazoches-sur-Guyonne, an hour's drive from Paris. He wanted to build a high-quality house that would act as both a family home and a space for his artworks, without the formality of a gallery. Carré initially approached Alvar Aalto in 1955 by letter and met him a year later at the 1956 Venice Biennale, where Aalto had designed the Finnish Pavilion. The pair instantly hit it off, and a lifelong friendship was born.

Aalto was tasked with designing every element of the house and garden, from the fixtures and furniture down to the light fittings and textiles. Carré's only request was that the building would not have a flat roof. Aalto agreed that a sloping roof would work better within the landscape, and aside from this he had a free hand.

The house sits high on top of a hill, with views right across the rural landscape. Its plan centres around a dramatic entrance hall with a free-form vaulted wooden ceiling. To the left of the entrance are the dining area and kitchen, and to the right steps lead down to the living space, with full-width south-facing windows. At the back are the bedrooms, bathrooms and sauna, and the upstairs was given over to the staff quarters. Externally the house is made of local stone and lime-washed brick, while the roof is of blue slate. It was completed in the main in 1959, but a number of additions, such as a heated pool and pool house, were built during the following years.

Maison Louis Carré is the only house in France by Alvar Aalto, and with much of it original it is a rare and excellent example of a complete work by the Finnish architect.

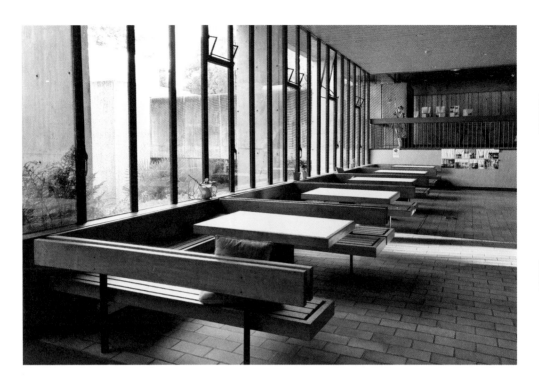

Moulin Blanc Youth Hostel

Architect

Roland Schweitzer

Year

1983

Location
5 Rue de Kerbriant
Brest 29200
France

aj-brest.org

The French architect and urban planner Roland Schweitzer, a former pupil of Auguste Perret and Jean Prouvé, became the National Council Architect of the Federation of Youth Hostels in the 1950s and worked on several hostels and holiday centres throughout his career. Although many are still standing — with some even listed as historical monuments — only a few have retained as much of their original character as the Moulin Blanc hostel in Brest, on the Brittany coast, completed in 1983.

Schweitzer was fascinated by Japanese and Scandinavian vernacular architecture and was particularly interested in wood. He admired the work of Alvar Aalto for its elegant use of natural materials, and in his designs Schweitzer applied a similarly rigorous and straightforward approach, combining concrete, glass and wood.

Built on the former property of the Count of Chalus, the hostel nestles amid lush greenery above the harbour. It comprises several buildings organised in a vast park. It exists harmoniously in its environment, sitting out of sight while simultaneously being fully open to the outside. The hostel offers a total of 136 beds, with four bunk-beds and a sink per room; three dining rooms of varying sizes; four meeting rooms; a large living room with a large fireplace; and a library area. A walkway connects the main buildings. Sleeping accommodation is positioned on the upper floors, while the communal spaces are at ground level. In the words of Marie Schweitzer, the architect's daughter, 'Spending a night in these rooms is a true experience of life. There's nothing superfluous in the rooms, nothing decorative: a sink, wooden beds each with a built-in lamp, recalling the world of boat crossings. It's an architecture that spans the ages without going out of style.'

Maison
Jean Prouvé

Architect

Jean Prouvé

Year

1954

Location
6 Rue Augustin Hacquard
Nancy 54100
France

musee-des-beaux-arts.
nancy.fr

Despite not having trained in engineering or architecture, Jean Prouvé showed remarkable skill in innovative construction methods and the understanding of materials. After studying at the École des Beaux-Arts in Nancy, Prouvé set up his first workshop in 1924, working on ornamental metalwork commissions. Towards the late 1920s he began to be interested in sheet metal and made a name for himself as a leader of modern techniques in metal, frequently collaborating with architects, including Le Corbusier.

With a sense of social welfare, Prouvé turned his attention to the country's housing shortage following the Second World War. He believed that the technological advances that were being utilised to make planes, cars and bridges should be used in architecture, and particularly in housing. In 1944 he was commissioned by the French state to design prefabricated, low-cost houses for the homeless that could be easily assembled.

By 1947 Prouvé had moved into a factory in nearby Maxéville, employing two hundred people. He refined and perfected his designs for factory-made housing, but unfortunately the profit margins were too small and a few years later he was forced to leave the business. During this time he bought a narrow plot of land in Nancy deemed too challenging to build on due to its steep slope. Here Prouvé showed his ingenuity by creating a single-storey house for himself; with the help of friends, the building, composed of standard materials such as sheet aluminium, went up in a matter of weeks. At the heart of the house is a large living room measuring 59 square metres, with a wall of glazing and views of the Nancy countryside. At one end of the building are the small yet functional bedrooms, and at the other is the kitchen. An office that had once stood in the Maxéville factory was erected in the garden.

The house and office can be visited on Saturday afternoons during the summer months, with tours conducted in French.

Villa Cavrois

Architect
Robert Mallet-Stevens

Year
1929–32

Location
60 Avenue du Président
John Fitzgerald Kennedy
Croix 59510
France

villa-cavrois.fr

Visiting the chateau-like Villa Cavrois today in its pristine condition, it is difficult to imagine it stood derelict and abandoned less than twenty years ago. Completed in 1932 and designed by Robert Mallet-Stevens, the villa has had a turbulent history. It was built for Paul Cavrois, a textile industrialist who had bought a plot of land in Croix, a bourgeois neighbourhood near Lille.

Mallet-Stevens, whose career focused on avant-garde film set design and private homes for affluent clients, was given a free hand as long as he kept within the (substantial) budget. The result was a thoroughly modern building with a long horizontal facade clad in sand-coloured brick, raising eyebrows among the conservative neighbours. The latest technologies, such as telephones, speakers and central heating, and luxurious materials, including Swedish green marble and Cuban mahogany, were incorporated. Adults and children were allocated separate zones — the children even had their own dining room. Mallet-Stevens designed most of the furniture and created rooms that looked like stylised theatre sets. Artificial and natural lighting plays a significant role in the interior, such as the expansive glazing in the living room or the impressive opal glass light-boxes by lighting designer André Salomon in the entrance hall.

The Cavrois fled the villa during the Second World War and German troops subsequently occupied it. When the family returned their needs had changed, and the couple commissioned architect Pierre Barbe to remodel the house, creating two self-contained apartments for their sons. The family lived here until 1986, and the following year it was sold to a developer and eventually fell into disrepair. In 2001 the state finally intervened and bought the property, entrusting it to the Centre des Monuments Nationaux. After twelve years of research and restoration to Mallet-Stevens's original design, one of his most significant works is open to the public.

Sainte-Marie de La Tourette

Architect

Le Corbusier

Year

1953–60

Location
Route de la Tourette
Éveux 69210
France

couventdelatourette.fr

Built between 1953 and 1960 in Éveux, 25 kilometres from Lyon, La Tourette was one of Le Corbusier's last and most important projects. It was commissioned by Father Marie-Alain Couturier, who requested a church, place of learning and residence for one hundred Dominican brothers. The complex is formed of two masses around a central courtyard: a rectangular box containing the church; and a U-shaped building comprising the common areas, which include study halls, work and recreation halls, and a library on the ground floor. On the lower level are the refectory and the cloister (in the form of a cross), leading to the church. The brothers' cells run around the perimeter of the building on the top two floors.

The rough reinforced concrete building looms large on a steeply sloping bank, a site chosen by Le Corbusier for its commanding views over the landscape. On approach, the building gives the illusion of defying gravity, unperturbed by the sloping ground beneath it, but it is in fact supported by tall concrete pilotis. The compact cells reflect the simplicity of monastic life and are equipped only with the essentials for sleeping and studying: a bed, a wash-basin, a desk and a lamp (almost identically to the hotel rooms in the Unité d'habitation in Marseille, see page 142). Each room has a balcony giving views towards the forest while also serving as protection from extreme weather. Fenestration is used to dramatic effect throughout the monastery. Long horizontal strips of glass run along the length of the corridors, and the refectory features large windows composed of rhythmic glazing. One of the most spectacular uses of natural light is in the church and crypt, where carefully placed 'light cannons' painted in red, blue and white project warm sunlight into the dark interior.

Now home to a much-reduced Dominican community of eleven friars, with the other rooms available for overnight stays, the monastery remains a popular spiritual retreat.

E-1027

Architect

Eileen Gray

Year

1929

and

Le Cabanon

Architect

Le Corbusier

Year

1951

Location
Sentier Massolin
Roquebrune-Cap-Martin
06190
France

capmoderne.com

Born into a bourgeois family in Ireland, Eileen Gray developed a lifelong passion for the Côte d'Azur when her mother took her to the south of France to recover from typhoid fever. She spent part of her childhood in London and later studied there at the Slade School of Fine Art before moving to Paris in 1902, where she remained for the rest of her life. By the early 1920s, Gray had become well recognised for her modern furniture designs, especially her work in lacquer.

Shortly after the First World War, Gray met the enthusiastic architecture critic Jean Badovici, and together they travelled across Europe looking at new buildings by leading modernist architects. A few years later he encouraged her to design him a summer house in the south of France. Gray made several site visits to the Côte d'Azur and finally found a perfect plot of land on a sloping site overlooking the sea in Roquebrune-Cap-Martin and bought it in Badovici's name. Without any previous experience or training, she set about designing the house, spending the next three years overseeing its construction. With meticulous attention to detail, she designed every aspect of the home, including ingenious free-standing and fitted multipurpose furniture — a number of these designs are still in production today. The building was completed in 1929, when Gray was 51 years old, and was an extraordinary achievement as her first building.

Despite its relatively small size the house feels spacious and light, with an effortless transition between indoor and outdoor. The space is logically organised: on the upper floor are two bedrooms, the kitchen and a large, rectangular open-plan living space with full-height and full-width glazing looking out towards the sea. Sailcloth awnings and deckchairs emphasise the maritime theme. An external staircase and an internal spiral staircase lead to the floor below, which comprises the guest and housekeeper's bedrooms. Gray had a passion for nature and gave equal attention

to the outdoor space and to working with the natural topography of the site, incorporating paths, a sunken seating area with table for drinks and even an outdoor kitchen to the north, sheltered by citrus trees. She moved out of the house a few years later and designed her own home, the Tempe à Pailla, in nearby Castellar.

Le Corbusier, a good friend of Badovici's, would often come to stay at the house. He wrote to Gray in admiration of her design, 'I am so happy to tell you how much those few days spent in your house have made me appreciate the rare spirit which dictates all the organisation inside and outside.' Controversially, however, in 1938 he persuaded Badovici to let him paint eight garish murals on its walls. A saddened Gray regarded this as an extreme act of vandalism from a man she admired. After the death of Badovici in 1956, the house began to deteriorate and was eventually abandoned and squatted. In the 1990s the villa was finally saved and extensive restoration work began. Having been returned to its former glory, it is now open to the public.

In 1950 Le Corbusier acquired a small plot of land next to E-1027 from Thomas Rebutato, proprietor of the nearby taverna Étoile de Mer. Here he built a tiny wooden shack for himself where he spent most of his summers. The simple mono-pitched *cabanon* is lined in plywood and clad in round logs. It measures a mere 3.66 by 3.66 metres, with a narrow corridor to one side; inside, it is simply equipped and designed in accordance with the architect's modular principles, with a bed, a cupboard, a table, some shelves and a WC. A few years later he designed the Unités de Camping —five holiday cabins—for Rebutato on the same site. In 1965, Le Corbusier died here of a heart attack during a morning swim.

Informative tours of the entire collection of buildings are available in either French or English.

Hotel
Le Corbusier

Architect

Le Corbusier

Year

1945

Location
Cité Radieuse
280 Boulevard Michelet
Marseille 13008
France

hotellecorbusier.com

The Cité Radieuse (Radiant City) in Marseille is possibly the most influential modernist residential building in the world and a site of architectural pilgrimage. It was listed as a UNESCO World Heritage Site in 2016. Many of its visitors come to stay in its hotel (initially designed for the residents' friends and family) for the first-hand experience of sleeping in a Le Corbusier design icon.

The devastation and housing shortage caused by the Second World War gave Le Corbusier the opportunity to put into practice his theories on the individual family dwelling, the grouping of dwellings, and the city, culminating in his first 'Unité d'habitation de grandeur conforme'. In this high-density megastructure — designed as a 'vertical city' — the architect united living, learning and recreation in a single structure. Situated in what was one of Marseille's most beautiful districts when completed in 1945, the imposing building is set within a park 5 kilometres from the city centre. The seventeen-storey slab has a length of 165 metres and a height of 56 metres and is raised off the ground on large pilotis. The gigantic reinforced concrete frame contains 337 structurally independent units inserted into a grid-like structure. The apartments are served by 'internal streets' on every third floor, with two levels of shopping facilities halfway up the building and the hotel occupying the third and fourth floors.

Communal facilities, including a roof terrace with sculptural ventilation stacks, a running track and a shallow pool, are accessible exclusively to the residents and hotel guests. As well as its 21 rooms the hotel also runs a gourmet restaurant. Room sizes range from the tiny yet authentic 'cabin' — similar to the monastic cells Le Corbusier designed at La Tourette (see page 138) — to large suites accommodating up to four people, each with a balcony featuring the architect's trademark concrete brise-soleil. They are furnished mostly with original pieces, including built-in furniture designed by Charlotte Perriand.

Hotel Les Cabanettes

Architect
Armand Pellier

Year
1965–67/ 1976–78

Location
D572N
Hameau Saliers
Arles 13200
France

lescabanettes.com

Until recently, the Hotel Les Cabanettes had been in the same family since its inception and maintained in astonishing original condition. When the tourism and leisure industry began to boom in the 1960s, hoteliers Louise and Marc Berc embarked on an ambitious project to build a hotel on a plot of land in Saliers, on the outskirts of the Camargue and 15 kilometres from Arles.

The Bercs were introduced to the sculptor and architect Armand Pellier, who shared their vision for a modern hotel. The open-minded couple entrusted Pellier with a flexible budget and high degree of design freedom, resulting in a rare piece of modernism that looks as if it has been plucked from Palm Springs and transported to rural France. It was a significant achievement for a single architect, and in recognition it is now classified as a twentieth-century heritage site by the French Ministry of Culture. The hotel is composed of three curved wings (completed in two stages), one housing the public spaces, including the reception, dining room and living room, and the other two containing the bedrooms (29 in total). The low, one-storey buildings are designed to integrate with the flat landscape; the only vertical element is the tall chimney of the dining room. Organic forms, natural materials such as local stone, textures of wood and rope, sculptural ironwork and furniture were all designed by Pellier and give this architectural gem a rich identity. Light and atmosphere are also carefully orchestrated: floor-to-ceiling windows in the public spaces open out to the landscape on the south sides, whereas, in contrast, the dimly lit curved corridors of the private zones are punctuated with small glass blocks placed at half-height.

In 2019 the hotel was taken over by Gaëlle and Aaron Redlin, who after working in the industry in New York and the south of France decided to embark on a new adventure. They are upgrading it to suit modern standards, yet retaining the unique character and spirit of the mid-century architecture they fell for.

Flaine

Architect
Marcel Breuer

Year
1969–76

Location
Flaine 74300
France

flaine.com

Totem hotel
totem.terminal-neige.com

After moving to the US in 1937, the Hungarian-born Bauhausler Marcel Breuer forged a successful career working on private house commissions as well as significant public works, including the St John's Abbey Church in Collegeville, Minnesota, and the UNESCO Headquarters in Paris.

In 1960 he was offered the unique opportunity to design and realise an entire town. The commission came via his friend and New Canaan neighbour Éric Boissonnas, who along with his brother Remi had the idea of building a new ski resort in Flaine, in the French Alps, an hour and a half's drive south from Geneva. The comprehensive brief included hotels, condominiums, row houses, chalets, a town hall, a cinema, ski jumps, a skating rink and ski school offices. The project was completed in two phases: the master plan was drawn up in 1961, and the buildings and subsequent phase were completed in 1976 in collaboration with American architect Robert Gatje. It was an incredibly ambitious project, not least because of the challenging mountain terrain and lack of roads to get to the 1,600-metre-high site.

To get around the problems of construction, many of the structures were prefabricated in concrete; aesthetically, this also helped integrate them into the mountain rock. The first building to be completed was the 4-star hotel Le Flaine (pictured opposite), whose cantilevered end dramatically juts out of the mountain rock and over the precipice. Although primarily a ski resort, Flaine was popular with tourists all year round. The resort also boasts sculptures by Jean Dubuffet, Victor Vasarely and Pablo Picasso.

The 1980s saw the public fall out of favour with concrete architecture, and the buildings became neglected and a shadow of their former selves. With the recent resurgence in brutalism, however, new life is being brought into the resort, including the newly renovated Totem hotel (pictured overleaf), which has been stylishly reborn as the Terminal Neige Totem.

Les Arcs

Architect
Charlotte Perriand

Year
1968

Location
Les Arcs
Bourg-Saint-Maurice 73700
France

lesarcs.com

Charlotte Perriand, best known for her furniture designs, began her career working with Le Corbusier. The fitted kitchens she designed for the Unité d'habitation in Marseille in the late 1940s epitomise her ambition to provide comfort, beauty and economy of space to the masses. It was not until she was in her sixties, however, that she embarked on her most significant project, the Les Arcs ski resort in Bourg-Saint-Maurice, southeast France.

Perriand loved fresh air and exercise, and when she returned to France from Japan after the war, finding a devastated Paris, she escaped to the French Alps, where she built herself a modest chalet in Méribel. The post-war years saw a growth in the popularity of leisure activities, particularly skiing. Roger Godino, an entrepreneur, developer and constructor in mountain tourism, saw what Perriand had achieved in her chalet and brought her on board as the chief architect of his new ski resort project. Together with Robert Blanc, a ski instructor and high mountain guide, they collaborated on a project that lasted over twenty years.

Perriand oversaw an enthusiastic team of architects to create three villages, Arc 1600, Arc 1800 and Arc 2000, each named according to their altitude. The first resort building, Les Trois Arcs, opened in 1968. Despite the structures being decidedly modern, Perriand skilfully integrated them into the natural landscape with minimal visual impact and no building overlooking another. Working on every aspect of the interiors, Perriand put her expertise in designing small spaces, mass production and local craftsmanship into practice to create functional rooms with practical built-in pine furniture. White walls are contrasted with the colourful, factory-built fibreglass bathrooms and kitchens, which were craned into place and quickly connected to the water and electricity supplies. Each apartment has large glazed doors that open out to the glorious landscape. Several still retain their original fittings today and can be rented out throughout the year.

Anderton House

Architect

Peter Aldington

Year

1971

Location
Goodleigh
Barnstaple
Devon EX32 7NR
UK

landmarktrust.org.uk

The Landmark Trust rescues vulnerable historic buildings that are in danger and sensitively restores them, giving them a new lease of life by making them available for holiday lets. The Anderton House, which the trust acquired in 2000, was its first modernist property. The Grade II* listed house (originally called Riggside) is one of the best-known designs by Peter Aldington, an influential architect of post-war domestic housing in Britain. It was commissioned in 1969 by his friends Ian and May Anderton, who wanted a small family home near Barnstable in North Devon for themselves and their daughter. The brief asked for a house that made the most of the views across the valley; a flexible open-plan living area suitable for cooking, eating, sitting and reading, with some demarcation; and three private and acoustically insulated bedrooms.

The single-storey house sits low on a sloping site, in keeping with the surrounding low farmhouses. Its use of a timber frame — prefabricated in Oxford under Aldington's supervision — and large areas of glazing gives the appearance that the roof floats above the walls. Quarry floor tiles in the living room extend to the outside, blurring the division between indoor and outdoor. A particular quirk of the house is what became nicknamed 'the doghouse'. Ian Anderton wanted an office area where he could work but still enjoy the views and be part of family life. The result was a shoulder-height, raised cubby in the centre of the living space, connected to all areas but allowing for clutter to be hidden within the enclosure.

The family were delighted with the result and lived here happily for the rest of their lives. The Anderton House remains instantly evocative of the 1970s and offers a unique opportunity to stay in one of the UK's most significant modern houses.

St Catherine's College

Architect
Arne Jacobsen

Year
1960–64

Location
University of Oxford
Manor Road
Oxford OX1 3UJ
UK

universityrooms.com

Founded in 1868, the St Catherine's Society assisted students studying at the University of Oxford who could not afford the high costs of college residence. In 1952 historian Alan Bullock was appointed head of the society and had the ambition to transform it into a large, modern residential college. During a trip to Copenhagen he visited several Arne Jacobsen buildings and was particularly impressed with his Munkegaard School in Vangede. On his return to the UK, Bullock commissioned the Danish architect to design the new college.

Jacobsen, initially ambivalent about the commission, was unfamiliar with what an Oxford college was. After studying the ground plans of the other colleges, he became inspired by the fourteenth-century New College, and his design for St Catherine's is a modern interpretation of the traditional college. At the heart of St Catherine's lies a rectangular quad with two long parallel residential blocks east and west, both three storeys high with glass facades. In between these are a further three blocks of buildings: a kitchen, offices, common rooms and the dining hall; the library; and an auditorium with a tall bell-tower. The gardens are an integral part of the overall concept. The design is dictated by the 3-metre grid that unifies the entire site, and it is divided by a series of spaces, or open-air 'rooms', defined by hedges, brick walls and covered walkways. Alongside the architecture, Jacobsen designed every aspect of the interior, including the furniture, light fittings, cutlery and door handles.

Outside term time, the college welcomes guests to stay in the dormitories. The rooms, with full-width and full-height glazing, are each equipped with a Jacobsen-designed desk, lamp, chair and built-in furniture. The monumental dining hall where breakfast is served, with its 6.5-metre-high ceiling and exposed construction, is particularly impressive.

The
Homewood

Architect
Patrick
Gwynne

Year
1938–39

Address
Portsmouth Road
Esher
Surrey KT10 9JL
UK

nationaltrust.org.uk

From 1913 the Gwynne family lived in a Victorian house in Esher, Surrey, with a large garden but close to the main road. The sound of the traffic was becoming unbearable, and 24-year-old Patrick Gwynne persuaded his parents to give him his first architectural commission—to design them a new house on the same plot but further back, away from the road. His parents agreed and gave him a very generous budget.

Taking inspiration from Le Corbusier's Villa Savoye (see page 128), the main rooms of the house are raised on pilotis, affording picturesque views of the garden. Internally, the influence of Mies van der Rohe is apparent in the extensive use of opulent materials such as terrazzo, marble and gold leaf. The ground level consists of an entrance lobby, a study, garage and servicing. Upstairs the building is split into two wings by a spiral staircase. On the east is the bedroom wing, and in the main wing is the living room and dining room, the kitchen and the staff quarters.

The outbreak of the Second World War would see the family leave the house. Unfortunately, Patrick Gwynne's parents died during the war, but he returned to the house and remodelled it for his own occupation, placing his architecture studio on the ground floor. He loved to entertain, and with its large open living room and maple floor—which would double up as a dance floor—The Homewood was the perfect location for hosting glamorous parties. The architect also designed much of the furniture, including a clever little fold-out bar discreetly hidden into the wall.

Gwynne lived in the house until his death in 2003, continually updating the decor through the decades, which makes it a rare example of a pre-war modernist house with continuity of occupation. He donated it along with the original furniture to the National Trust, and it has been open to the public since 2004 for tours during the summer months.

Vista Point

Architect
Patrick Gwynne

Year
1969–70

Location
Tamarisk Way
East Preston
West Sussex BN16 2TE
UK

vista-point.co.uk

Unlike most of his contemporaries in post-war Britain, who sought work in the public sector, architect Patrick Gwynne focused his attention on designing private homes for wealthy clients. In the late 1960s he was commissioned by his quantity surveyor, Kenneth Monk, to design a holiday home. Vista Point (originally named Monk House), complete with a swimming pool and pool house, is situated immediately on the seafront in East Preston, on the Sussex coast in the south of England. Gwynne was unimpressed with the architecture of the surrounding houses and so positioned the house to face inwards, towards the garden. It is worth noting, however, that the Sea Lane House designed by Bauhaus master Marcel Breuer is only a ten-minute walk away.

The two-storey Vista Point has an 'hourglass' plan and at its core is a dramatic ash-panelled spiral staircase with a dome skylight. On the ground floor are five bedrooms and three bathrooms, which wrap around the central core and neatly divide the house into two wings—one initially intended for guests and the other for the Monks. Gwynne positioned the main living spaces upstairs, exploiting the sea views. The design of the balcony off the living room gives it a nautical theme.

Gwynne paid meticulous attention to detail. For example, he used materials that would withstand the harsh marine environment, such as the Mineralite exterior rendering (a durable material that glitters in the sun); the corrugated white plastic fascia; and the garden screen metalwork, coated with rubber. Fifty years on, Vista Point remains in remarkably good condition.

The Monks sold the house in 1972, and since then it has had a handful of owners, but each has respected and cherished the original design and much of it is unaltered, including the turquoise, navy and yellow Pop-coloured bathrooms and the unique built-in furniture. The house was Grade II listed in 2006 and today is available as a holiday home throughout the year.

Ellis-Miller House

Architect

Jonathan Ellis-Miller

Year

1992

Location
Kingdon Avenue
Prickwillow
Ely
Cambridgeshire CB7 4UL
UK

bestofsuffolk.co.uk

Situated in the village of Prickwillow, 6 kilometres outside the city of Ely and overlooking the Cambridgeshire Fens, the Ellis-Miller House is an elegant steel-framed pavilion reminiscent of the Californian Case Study Houses of the 1940s and 1950s. Its front elevation is made entirely of glass sliding panels, making the most of the spectacular views.

It was designed in the late 1980s by Norfolk-born architect Jonathan Ellis-Miller, who at the time worked for the eminent architect John Winter (see page 166). Ellis-Miller wanted to create a low-cost self-build house to use as a weekend retreat. The compact building, with a footprint of just 66 square metres, is made up of three bays: a study area and bedroom, a living area and kitchen, and a carport. Recently, however, the study and living area have been opened up to make a single open-plan space.

Due to the treacherous ground conditions of the Fens, Ellis-Miller sought a lightweight construction solution so that a reinforced concrete raft foundation could be used instead of costly piling. The architect endeavoured wherever possible to use simple, honest materials that could be on display rather than hidden. As an alternative to using timber studs for non-load-bearing walls, for example, a galvanised steel structural roof doubles up as a ceiling finish.

The house received two prominent prizes, the RIBA National Award and the British Steel Award, both in 1993. It recently came under new ownership and, since much of its original low-cost construction needing updating, underwent a sympathetic refurbishment. It is now available as a holiday let for a minimum of three nights. Also worthy of interest is the house next door, again designed by Ellis-Miller, initially for the artist Mary Banham, wife of the architecture critic Reyner Banham.

Frinton Park Estate

Architect
Oliver Hill

Year
1935

Location
Warley Way
Frinton-on-Sea
Essex CO13 9PA
UK

frintonholidaylets.com

While the 1930s saw the construction of uncompromising modernist housing schemes across mainland Europe, England was also embracing the International Style, albeit on a smaller scale. There are pockets on the outskirts of London, and in Essex in particular, that are home to a surprising number of flat-roofed, white-rendered interwar houses.

The Frinton Park Estate, in the small seaside town of Frinton-on-Sea, constitutes the largest group of individually designed modernist houses in the UK. In 1934 the South Coast Investment Company bought a 200-acre plot of land and commissioned Oliver Hill to create a master plan for 1,100 homes, a shopping centre and a hotel. Hill, along with Frederick Etchells, R. A. Duncan and Marshall Sisson, designed 25 show homes to entice prospective clients to purchase a plot and commission a house from a list of architects. The list included Serge Chermayeff, Tecton, Wells Coates, F.R.S. Yorke, Maxwell Fry and Connell, Ward & Lucas. Despite the ambitious plan, only an additional fifteen houses were eventually realised, their modern design perhaps too radical for conservative England. Their construction relied on contractors unfamiliar with new building methods and designs, which caused problems, not least with the flat roofs. Hill left the project in 1935, and the developers took over.

Of the forty built, this particular house, designed by Hill, received a great deal of press and was featured in several publications. Situated above cliffs only a few hundred feet from the beach, it was initially intended as a holiday home and is now available to rent. The structure comprises two storeys and features an impressive curved living room with sweeping ribbon Crittall windows and parquet flooring. Upstairs are five bedrooms, three of which have a sun deck. Modern additions include the conversion of the garage into a summer dining room with direct access to an outdoor pool.

Beach House

Architect
John Winter

Year
1990

Location
Doggett's Lane
Happisburgh
Norwich
Norfolk NR12 0QL

beachhousenorfolk.co.uk

After spending an influential period in the USA studying at Yale University under Louis Kahn and working for Skidmore, Owings & Merrill and Charles Eames, British architect John Winter returned to the UK in the late 1950s and set about designing and building his own house. During this hands-on process Winter learnt skills such as bricklaying and concrete shuttering. He went on to create two further homes for his own family — the famous Cor-Ten steel Grade II* listed house on Swain's Lane in Highgate, London, in 1967 and the Beach House in Happisburgh on the Norfolk coast in 1990.

The plot of land on which the Beach House sits had previously housed an older dwelling where Winter, his wife Valerie — a graphic artist and garden designer — and their three children would holiday. With the collapse of nearby cliffs, the house was in danger of disappearing, so the Winters chose to demolish it and build a new building set further back. The design of the new holiday home comprises a modest structure with steel and aluminium profile sheets supported by a lightweight steel frame, sitting low among the dunes. The house is essentially a rectangle in plan, divided into three sections. At one end is the entrance and the bathroom, with a delightful little porthole window that allows views of the outside from the bath. The middle bay is an open-plan area comprising the kitchen, dining and living room with a sunken conversation pit and a log burner; and at the furthest end is a double bedroom and a carport. The Winters had to sacrifice the sea view in favour of shelter from the harsh Norfolk shore by incorporating a protective garden designed by Valerie.

The Beach House accommodates two guests, with an adjacent wooden chalet sleeping a further four.

2 Willow Road

Architect
Ernő Goldfinger

Year
1939

Location
2 Willow Road
London NW3 1TH
UK

nationaltrust.org.uk

A visit to 2 Willow Road, one of the earliest modernist houses in the UK, is a unique opportunity to experience a home complete with all of its original content and to sense how its architect, Ernő Goldfinger, and his family once lived. Budapest-born Goldfinger settled in London in 1934 and initially lived in Berthold Lubetkin's Highpoint flats in Highgate before moving to Hampstead. Financing from his wife, Ursula Blackwell—heir to the Crosse & Blackwell food company—enabled Goldfinger to design and build a home that could also act as a showpiece for his vision and skills as an architect.

The fact that a few small cottages on the site, on the edge of Hampstead Heath in north London, had to be demolished to make way for the new terrace of three houses prompted great local opposition. Goldfinger assured the planners that little concrete would be on show and that the building would be faced with red brick, in keeping with the surrounding architecture, and so planning permission was finally granted.

The houses were completed in 1939, with the middle and largest designed for the Goldfingers. Spatially the home has a traditional layout, with the living room on the first floor, the bedrooms and bathrooms on the second, and the kitchen and servants' rooms on the ground floor and basement. The reinforced concrete frame, with exposed load-bearing columns, allowed for a free plan and spacious, open interiors. A stretch of continuous glazing spans all three houses. The sculptural spiral staircase inside a concrete drum acts as a supporting column in the centre of the house. Much of the furniture, such as the innovative built-in cabinets, desk and dining table, was designed by Goldfinger. One of the highlights of the house is the impressive collection of artworks by the couple's friends and contemporaries, including Bridget Riley, Henry Moore and Man Ray. The house is owned and managed by the National Trust, who offer regular tours.

Chert

and

Little Chert

Architects

Gilbert
& Hobson

Year

1967–70

Location
Castle Court
Ventnor
Isle of Wight PO38 1UE
UK

nationaltrust.org.uk

The National Trust sensitively restored the Chert house after acquiring it in 1995, and since 2000 it has been available to rent as a holiday cottage. It was designed in 1967 as a retirement house for two professional women, Koo Haddock MBE and Connie McDowell. With their combined technical knowledge—Haddock had been an engineer at the Ministry of Aviation and McDowell a doctor of chemistry—the women decided to design the house themselves, employing local architects Gilbert & Hobson to follow their design.

The two-storey building is built into the cliff at Ventnor on the Isle of Wight and is composed of two symmetrical wings, one for each woman. It is constructed in concrete, timber weatherboarding and brick. On the ground floor are two garages either side of the entrance, and the cantilevered top floor is accessed via a spiral staircase. The living space has glazing running along its full length, with views towards the sea. Each wing comprised two reception rooms, a bathroom and a kitchen and had no bedrooms as such, just a daybed in each of the living rooms. The women shared the sun deck, which spans the width of the house.

Internally, many of the original features remain, including the built-in furniture, colourful kitchens with an innovative Formica fold-down breakfast table, and mosaics and tiles created by the owners. Some of the free-standing furniture is also original, while other items are reproductions in keeping with the 1970s aesthetic. There are now two bedrooms, sleeping up to four people. Next to the main house, also designed by Haddock and McDowell, is Little Chert—a single storey 'mini-me' building intended as a guest annexe for two people and also available to rent through the National Trust.

House Van Wassenhove

Architect
Juliaan Lampens

Year
1974

Location
50 Brakelstraat
Sint-Martens-Latem 9830
Belgium

museumdd.be

Until the 1960s Juliaan Lampens designed housing in a traditional Belgian style, using red brick and gabled roofs. However, the World's Fair of 1958, held in Brussels, made a profound impact on him, and when he came to design his own house a few years later he made a radical departure in style, favouring sculptural forms in raw cast concrete, drawing inspiration from Second World War bunkers.

Albert Van Wassenhove, a single and somewhat solitary man but an enthusiast of modern art and architecture, visited Lampens's Kerselare Chapel in Oudenarde and fell in love with the architecture. In 1972 he commissioned Lampens to design a house in Sint-Martens-Latem, near Ghent, giving him almost carte blanche. As with many of Lampens's homes, it is closed off to the public on one side but completely open to nature on the other. Fortress-like concrete walls shield the front from the street, while at the back, large glazed doors open out to a tranquil garden. Wanting to free its inhabitants from the restrictions of rooms, and inspired by primitive housing types, the architect did away with internal walls, encouraging families to live together in one open space, without the usual hierarchy. The compact plan of the Van Wassenhove house is contained within a U-shaped concrete shell across two half-floors. Geometric shapes define different zones: the sleeping area is a 1.5-metre-high wooden cylinder; the kitchen extractor hood a concrete triangle; and the office is placed within a square. Apart from the sleeping cylinder and the pine floor, the entire house is made from rough-cast concrete.

After the death of Van Wassenhove in 2012, the house was bequeathed to the University of Ghent, which in turn gave it on long-term loan to the local Dhondt-Dhaenens museum. Architecture enthusiasts are now able to experience one of Lampens's most important works at first hand, with short stays available during the summer months.

Joris Lens House

Architect

Huib Hoste

Year

1934

Location
7 Schuttersvest
Mechelen 2800
Belgium

facebook.com/
Huib-Hoste-384899518519914

Situated in the small city of Mechelen, which lies between Brussels and Antwerp, the Joris Lens House is a uniquely intact house by Huib Hoste, one of the most important Belgian architects of the modern movement.

Joris Lens, a lawyer, commissioned Hoste in the early 1930s to design a family house that would incorporate an office for his law firm. Making use of the awkward site, on the upper floors Hoste created a slanting facade which he projected beyond the footprint of the site, so that the interior spaces would be rectangular. This allowed him to position the front door into the side of the building, rather than opening up directly on to the road. The law practice was located on the ground floor; the dining, kitchen and living spaces placed on the first floor; the bedrooms and bathroom on the second; and at the top is a further bedroom, a study and a sun terrace.

The house was created with maximum practicality in mind. Built-in furniture—such as nifty two-way cupboards that are accessible from both the kitchen and dining room—as well as bespoke free-standing pieces were all designed by Hoste. A broad combination of colours and textures, such as woods, ceramics and textiles, adorns the house and gives it a rich and comfortable feel. In contrast, the facade is rendered in white cimorné plaster (a finish composed of cement render with opalescent glass granules), perforated with large, black-painted metal window frames.

The house is only in its second ownership: a testament to the success of the design. The current owner, an architect, has gone to great lengths to restore it to its original design and colour scheme, including acquiring a vast collection of authentic Hoste furniture pieces. It is open to the public on occasion and to groups by special appointment.

Schellekens House

Architect
Jozef Schellekens

Year
1934

Location
Steenweg op Mol 66
Turnhout 2300
Belgium

centrum.ar-tur.be

The introduction of modernist architecture to the small Belgian town of Turnhout began when Jozef Schellekens designed an ultra-modern double house for his own family and his friend the writer Theo Op de Beeck in 1934. Constructed in brick with clean lines, large areas of glazing and a flat roof, it is today regarded as one the most important early modernist buildings in the Kempen region. Inside, cubic volumes of varying height and size define the living spaces. When completed in 1935, the house's modern appearance came under attack from local residents for being too radical.

A few years later, Jozef Schellekens became the provincial architect of Turnhout, designing public buildings such as schools and town halls and overseeing various restoration projects following the Second World War. Now protected as a Flemish monument, the house remains in the hands of the Schellekens family. Its interior, with original brightly coloured walls, has been carefully restored along with the unique built-in furniture. It is open to the public on occasion as part of architecture tours organised by AR-TUR.

Continuing the legacy of modernist architecture in Turnhout, in 1964 Schellekens's son Paul and son-in-law Carli Vanhout founded the architecture practice Atelier Vanhout & Schellekens (see page 180).

Veado

Architect
Paul Schellekens

Year
1969

Location
8 Hertenstraat
Turnhout 2300
Belgium

veado.be

During the 1960s three young architecture practices, Paul Neefs, Atelier Vanhout & Schellekens, and the office of Lou Jansen and Rudi Schiltz, began to make their mark in Turnhout. Although each had their individual style, the architects were influenced by the likes of Le Corbusier, Oscar Niemeyer, Arne Jacobsen, Hans Scharoun and Ludwig Mies van der Rohe. The architects worked on several projects throughout the town and beyond, including private houses, monasteries, offices and shops as well as their own family houses, and their output is now counted as among the best post-war architecture in Flanders. The style was later dubbed the Turnhoutse School by eminent Belgian architect Renaat Braem.

Carli Vanhout's impressive home and studio on Parklaan, completed in 1964, is now the office of Architects in Motion, founded by Vanhout's son Luc in 2002. Paul Schellekens's house, constructed in 1969, has recently been converted into a bed and breakfast. The building is essentially one large roof structure, covered with a patchwork of windows and with its gable practically touching the ground on both sides. The interior is a labyrinth of spaces with vistas running across all three floors. The use of exposed beams, brick walls and carefully positioned glazing gives the house a sense of warmth, while white ceilings are punctuated with bold colours. Schellekens lived in the house until 2006. Its current owners have renamed it Veado and, abiding by its listed status, have sympathetically updated the house, bringing it in line with twenty-first-century standards and offering three modern bedrooms, with breakfast in the original 'winter garden'.

Renaat Braem House and Studio

Architect
Renaat Braem

Year
1958

Location
23 Menegemlei
Antwerp 2100
Belgium

expeditiedestad.be

The Renaat Braem House and Studio is situated in the Deurne area of Antwerp, approximately 4 kilometres from the centre of the city. It was designed in 1958 by architect Renaat Braem for his own use. Braem was one of the most notable Belgian figures of twentieth-century modernism and began his career as an assistant to Le Corbusier in the 1930s.

The house stands at the end of a row of houses, and the street-facing facade is a stark wall of bricks, blind except for a garage door and three stacked vertical windows on the left-hand side. A ramp leads from the road up to the garage, while the front door is tucked discreetly into the side of the building. In contrast to the front, the side and rear facades are fragmented with a grid of glazing. The pattern continues into the steel parapets of the roof terraces and the open framework that visually encloses the space of the roof garden.

A constructivist-style staircase defines the plan of the house and runs over four floors. The building is broadly divided into two, with an architecture studio occupying the lower levels and living quarters on the upper two floors. Braem used colour, material and texture to define spaces, functions and atmosphere. Light colours and large windows, for example, were placed on the south-facing side of the building, where Braem positioned the dining area and his studio. Darker, richer colours were used on the north side to enclose cosier spaces such as the snug. The house and studio are filled with artefacts from all over the world, as well as personal items the architect collected during his travels. Particularly impressive is a wall of wooden objects in his office which also doubles as sound insulation. In 1999 Braem donated his home and its entire contents to the Flemish Community, and it is now run as a living museum, open to the public through guided tours.

Diagoon

Architect

Herman Hertzberger

Year

1970–71

Location
Gebbenlaan
Delft 2625
Netherlands

diagoonwoningdelft.nl

The Diagoon housing scheme is situated in Delft, 14 kilometres north of Rotterdam. It was designed by prominent Dutch architect Herman Hertzberger in the late 1960s and was initially conceived as a much larger scheme comprising 324 family houses. The project, however, became too much of a risk financially and was scaled back to twelve units, and eventually only eight dwellings were realised.

The concept for these experimental houses should be understood in the context of the mass public housing projects that were being built across post-war Europe. These were often standardised units offering little individualism—Hertzberger wanted to offer something different. He believed users should have the freedom to decide for themselves how to organise their homes. In the Diagoon houses, only the shell, the central staircase and the wet areas (bathroom and kitchens) are fixed. L-shaped split-level floors of equal size wrap around a central void, but exactly how the homes were to be used or divided was left to the inhabitants. The architect suggested 32 variations for how they could be planned—from a single space to one divided into four smaller, independent units sharing a communal centre. Even the roof terrace could be covered and transformed into another living unit. Familiar materials such as concrete blocks (internally and externally), wood and glass were used to encourage the residents to participate in the completion of the construction.

The original owner of number 32 remained in the house until 2011. A few years later it was bought by the architect Robert von der Nahmer, who on seeing it immediately knew that he wanted to live in this pioneering housing scheme. Apart from necessary upgrading, such as structural repairs and improving sustainability, no significant changes have been made and the home remains true to the original design. Von der Nahmer offers tours of his home by prior appointment.

Dijkstra House

Architects

Ben
Merkelbach

and

Charles
Karsten

Year

1933

Location
2 Nieuweweg
Groet 1871
Netherlands

monumentenbed.nl

Intended as a summer residence for a lawyer and his family, the Dijkstra House was designed in 1933 by Ben Merkelbach and Charles Karst — leading architects of the Dutch Nieuwe Bouwen style. Since fresh air and visits to the seaside were widely considered to be beneficial to one's health and well-being in the 1930s, the Dijkstras decided on a plot of land a few kilometres from the beach and dunes of the Schoorlse Duinen national park in North Holland.

The two-storey detached building, built of brick with steel windows and a flat roof, has a compact footprint of just 6 by 9 metres. Its layout centres on practical living — light, air, sun and visual contact with the environment were critical to the design. Large sliding doors in the living room swing out to form wind shields and connect the house to the surrounding landscape. The small yet rational kitchen is reminiscent of the ones designed by Le Corbusier at the Weissenhof Estate in Stuttgart, Germany. The straightforward floor plan comprises an L-shaped living room, kitchen and WC on the ground floor, while on the first floor are four bedrooms, two of which have access to a full-width balcony on the southeast side, and a shower. The interior colour palette — grey tones in combination with bright blue in the kitchen, yellow on the stairs and the sofas in the living room, white ceilings and off-white walls — was chosen in consultation with the architects and the painter Wim Schuhmacher, a friend of the Dijkstras.

The Dijkstra House and its contents were acquired by the Hendrick de Keyser Association in 2012. Since 1918 the association has been safeguarding Dutch houses of historical and architectural value, several of which are available as holiday homes through the organisation's dedicated website 'Monument and Bed' (see also page 194). With accommodation for up to six people this unique summerhouse can now be rented for a minimum of one week.

Rietveld Schröder House

Architect

Gerrit Rietveld

Year

1924

Location
50 Prins Hendriklaan
Utrecht 3583
Netherlands

rietveldschroderhuis.nl

Occupying a corner plot on what was formerly the edge of the city of Utrecht, the Rietveld Schröder House, constructed in 1924, was commissioned by the recently widowed Truus Schröder-Schräder, who needed a smaller house for herself and her three children. Having worked with the furniture designer Gerrit Rietveld in the past, and sharing a similar vision of what a modern house should be, she entrusted Rietveld with the design of her new home.

Rietveld was already well known for his furniture designs, in particular his famous Red and Blue Chair. The Rietveld Schröder House, however, would be his first entire house commission and one that allowed him the freedom to fully realise the ideas of the De Stijl movement. The two-storey house is in complete accordance with the movement, as expressed in the strong horizontal and vertical lines and primary colours against white, grey and black.

The architect placed the kitchen-dining room, studio, reading room and a sleeping area on the ground floor, while upstairs are the bedrooms and bathroom and a living-dining area with an ingenious corner window that swings open, dissolving the entire corner so that the indoors suddenly becomes the outdoors. The first floor was initially designed with standard walls dividing the rooms, but Schröder suggested making it completely open plan by removing all of the partitions. Rietveld loved the idea and devised several innovative sliding and folding walls that allow the space to be open in the day and closed off for privacy in the evenings.

Schröder lived in the house until her death in 1985, and it is now managed and maintained by the Centraal Museum, who organise regular guided tours. Almost everything is in its original state, having been carefully restored, including the furniture positioned as it was in the 1920s.

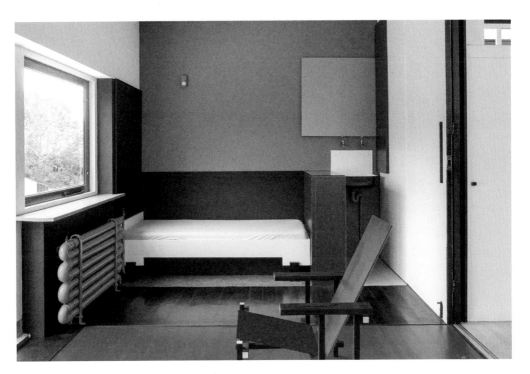

The Rietveld Schröder House initially backed on to rolling countryside. This beautiful view played an essential part in the design of the house, and to ensure nothing would get built in front of it Schröder-Schräder bought the land opposite when it became earmarked for redevelopment in the early 1930s. Once again she asked Gerrit Rietveld to design the project: a block of four townhouses, completed in 1931, and an apartment block, completed in 1934. The development, known as Erasmuslaan, differs in style from his earlier project. The primary colours typical of the De Stijl movement, seen in the Rietveld Schröder House, are absent; instead the architect moved to the principles of the Nieuwe Bouwen, favouring white plastered walls and steel window frames. There are, however, similarities in the flexibility of space, such as the partitions used on the ground floor.

In October 1931, Rietveld and Schröder furnished one of the houses to serve as a model home. The Centraal Museum has reconstructed this interior and it is now open to the public. Additionally, the museum has furnished an apartment at Robijnhof, a social housing scheme designed by Rietveld in Utrecht's Tolsteeg district.

Sybold van Ravesteyn House

Architect

Sybold van Ravesteyn

Year

1932–34

Location
112 Prins Hendriklaan
Utrecht 3584
Netherlands

monumentenbed.nl

When the architect Sybold van Ravesteyn graduated from the Delft technical institute in 1912, he began his career working as an engineer for Dutch State Railways. He later became known for his work designing elegant functionalist glass signal boxes on slim concrete columns, aligning with the doctrine of the De Stijl movement and later the Nieuwe Bouwen style. In the 1930s, following a trip to Italy, his work reached a turning point. He became influenced by Baroque architecture and shifted to a more idiosyncratic style, distancing himself from his Dutch contemporaries; his friend and De Stijl member Gerrit Rietveld, however, remained supportive.

Van Ravesteyn's home in Utrecht, on the same street as the Rietveld Schröder House (see page 192), is an exercise in curves, perspective and illusion. The building, constructed between 1932 and 1934, sits on a triangular, tapered plot of land whose awkward shape dictated the need for a non-standard structure. The modest building in sand-coloured brick consists of a rectangular two-storey volume and a semicircular volume with its first-floor facade set back to allow for a large roof terrace. The house combines neo-Baroque curved lines and ornament with the idiom of modernism—efficiency of space through modest means and modern materials. The large open-plan ground-floor space acted as a single room for daily activities—sitting, dining and working—with the delineation in functions suggested by the curved lines in the floor, a wing-shaped suspended ceiling of frosted glass in a steel frame, and built-in or fixed furniture. The house, intended as a family residence for the architect and his second wife, who was pregnant at the time of its design, has three bedrooms on the first floor. Van Ravesteyn lived here until he was in his nineties, and the Hendrick de Keyser Association acquired it in 2006. After an extensive renovation, the building was opened as a house museum and is now also available for overnight stays.

Sonneveld House

Architect

Brinkman & Van der Vlugt

Year

1929–33

Locations
12 Jongkindstraat
Rotterdam 3015
Netherlands

sonneveldhouse.com

Sonneveld House is one of the best examples of a fully furnished home in the Dutch functionalist style, known as Nieuwe Bouwen, that is open to the public for self-guided tours. This large home is situated in the centre of Rotterdam; although now a built-up area, it would have been surrounded by beautiful countryside when constructed. It was designed by Brinkman & Van der Vlugt and commissioned by Albertus Sonneveld, director of the Van Nelle tobacco factory, and his wife, Gésine, for themselves and their two daughters. Sonneveld, inspired by his trips to America and stays in luxury hotels, wanted a house that was truly modern, functional, hygienic and luxurious with all modern conveniences. The architects worked closely with their clients to ensure that the house suited their particular lifestyle; music speakers and telephones, for example, were installed in every room.

The three-storey reinforced concrete building has bands of windows running the length of the front and back, with doors opening to the large garden that surrounds it. The ground floor houses the garage (now used as an exhibition space to tell the house's history), the servants' apartment and a garden room for the Sonnevelds' daughters, which features a wooden floor—most probably for dancing. On the first floor is a large open space that can be subdivided with sliding doors to separate the living, library and dining areas. Additionally there is large utilitarian kitchen with innovative gadgets, including an electric coffee grinder. On the second floor are the bedrooms and exceptionally luxurious bathrooms. Colour plays an integral part in the interior, with warm, bright colours such as vermilion, cornflower blue and canary yellow combined with light and dark grey and brown.

The family, whose previous home was a nineteenth-century townhouse, decided to take none of their old furniture with them and furnished their new home with modern pieces by leading contemporary designers and manufacturers such as Gispen.

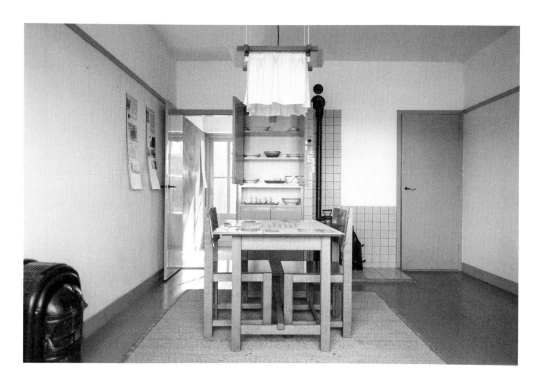

Kiefhoek

Architect

J.J.P. Oud

Year

1925–30

Location
2 Hendrik Idoplein
Rotterdam 3073
Netherlands

urbanguides.nl

The Dutch architect J.J.P. Oud was one of the original members of the De Stijl movement. Between 1918 and 1922 he was Municipal Housing Architect for Rotterdam and gained an international reputation for his pioneering functionalist architecture for modern living. As with many of his contemporaries, Oud was interested in tackling the housing shortage and concentrated on designing small, low-cost dwellings for the most impoverished families. During the slum clearances of the mid-1920s, the Kiefhoek neighbourhood in the Feijenoord district of south Rotterdam left an awkward site that was earmarked for homes for less prosperous families. Oud approached the project pragmatically and aimed to produce low-cost housing by employing the same industrialised techniques used in mass car manufacturing.

Created on an extremely tight budget, the finished scheme comprised 294 low-rise terraced houses with a standardised plan, two shops, a boiler house, a children's play area, a communal garden and a church. Despite the homes' extremely compact size, Oud maximised their interiors with simple, functional and well-lit spaces—for example, the living rooms have full-width windows, and even the stairwells are brightly lit. The homes were furnished with space-saving built-in elements such as cupboards, a small fireplace and coat rack. The upstairs spaces, intended to accommodate families of up to two adults, three daughters and three sons, are divided into four areas: three bedrooms and a space at the top of the landing for storage and drying clothes. Bright paint colours, seen in the yellow window frames, red doors and blue gates, were used as an inexpensive way of adding character to the otherwise white facades, and small front gardens allowed the residents to personalise their homes. When completed, the overall design of the scheme was greeted with international acclaim. Tours of the estate start at the Kiefhoek House Museum.

Van Eesteren Museum Apartment

Architects

Nielsen, Spruit & Van der Kuilen

Year

1952

Location
27 Freek Oxstraat
Amsterdam 1063
Netherlands

vaneesterenmuseum.nl

By the beginning of the twentieth century, Amsterdam's living conditions for most ordinary people had become deplorable, resulting in the Housing Act of 1917, which required councils to draw up expansion plans with provisions for public housing. The first to be realised was Plan Zuid (South Plan), with housing schemes in the Amsterdam School style: typically red brick buildings in expressive forms, such the Dageraad complex by Michel de Klerk and Piet Kramer in Amsterdam-Zuid. The Amsterdam School building method, however, was too expensive to be extended on a large scale, and in 1935, still faced with a housing shortage, the new General Extension Plan was drawn up.

The architect and urban planner largely responsible for the new plan was Cornelis van Eesteren, widely known for his contribution to the De Stijl movement and as the chairman of CIAM. He developed a 'functionalist city' concept of town planning, of which he commented: 'Our residential and working centres ought to be laid out and built with respect to needs, to life itself, that is to say, they must meet demands relating to hygiene, employment opportunities, traffic, leisure etc.' During the post-war period he introduced the garden city approach to housing, developing the district west of Amsterdam's ring road — which became known as Westelijke Tuinsteden, or Western Garden Cities — using a range of typologies, including slab blocks with gallery access, point blocks and row houses.

In 2012 the local Van Eesteren Museum opened a house museum in a restored apartment on Freek Oxstraat, complete with 1950s period furnishings and decorated following the principles of the Stichting Goed Wonen (Association for Good Living). The association was set up after the Second World War to bring together idealistic architects, designers, manufacturers, shopkeepers and consumers to promote well-designed domestic goods. Guided tours of the apartment are conducted in Dutch.

Bridge Houses SWEETS Hotels

Architect
Various

Year
Various

Location
28 locations across
Amsterdam
Netherlands

sweetshotel.amsterdam

For over one hundred years, Amsterdam's bridgemasters, responsible for opening and closing bridges for passing boat traffic across the city's 100 kilometres of canals, were accommodated in bridge houses—little structures perched on bridges, giving panoramic views of the surroundings. With the introduction of modern automated systems the buildings have become redundant, and since 2018 these tiny buildings have been adapted to create modern hotel rooms accommodating up to two people. Each bridge house has been renovated by design agency Space&Matter, who came up with the concept in 2010. The architects have cleverly maximised the spaces while respecting the architecture of the structures, some of which are listed.

Constructed over a lengthy time span, from the early twentieth century's Amsterdam School period to recent eye-catching structures by contemporary architects, the bridge houses reflect the changing architectural movements of Amsterdam. Of the 28 buildings, several are in the modernist style, built in the 1950s and 1960s when the architect Dirk Sterenberg was in charge of the city's Bridges Division. Sterenberg, clearly inspired by the Nieuwe Bouwen movement, used expanses of glass, steel and concrete, as expressed in the Hortusbrug bridge house he designed in 1956 (pictured on page 204). Located close to the botanical garden in central Amsterdam, the concrete T-shaped building with two striking cantilevers appears to float on water. The exterior is painted white with dark steel window frames, while its painted blue panels are reminiscent of the work of Gerrit Rietveld. Other buildings constructed during this period include the 1965 Gerben Wagenaarbrug bridge house in Kraaienplein, a tall brick tower with a band of horizontal glazing, designed by Enrico Hartsuyker; and the cylinder-shaped Kortjewantsbrug house on Prins Hendrikkade, designed in 1967 by Dick Slebos (pictured on page 205).

Tautes Heim

Architect

Bruno Taut

Year

1925–30

Location
Hufeisensiedlung
Berlin 12359
Germany

tautes-heim.de

Following its defeat in the First World War, Germany was left economically devastated and faced a severe housing shortage — in Berlin alone an estimated 140,000 new homes were needed. In order to tackle the crisis, the government placed a 15 per cent tax on rents to fund the building of new homes, but the state alone did not have the capacity to build in such high quantities, and housing associations such as GEHAG helped to meet the target. GEHAG's founder was the architect and town planner Martin Wagner, Berlin's chief city planner from 1926 to 1933. Along with his colleague Bruno Taut, he was committed to solving the housing problems the city faced. Inspired by the garden city movement, GEHAG and Taut were responsible for creating thousands of light and airy dwellings, with access to green spaces, across Berlin.

The Hufeisensiedlung (Horseshoe Estate), designed by Taut in 1925 and situated in Britz, a southeastern suburb of Berlin, is one of eight schemes declared a UNESCO World Heritage site in 2008 for representing 'a new type of social housing from the period of classical modernity'. A dramatic continuous U-shaped apartment building, with a pond dating back to the ice age at its centre, dominates the Hufeisensiedlung, with streets radiating from it lined with flat-roofed houses and apartment blocks. Taut used a palette of bold contrasting colours such as blues, yellows and reds, both externally and internally, as an inexpensive way to add character and to avoid monotony.

The architect devised cost-effective, standardised rational floor plans across the estate to minimise the construction costs and therefore the rents. Since 2012 one of the two-bedroom houses has been available to let as a holiday home with accommodation for up to four people. Its owners — a landscape architect and a designer who already lived on the estate — have immaculately and sensitively restored the house and have received several heritage awards for their restoration work.

Oscar-Niemeyer-Haus

Architect

Oscar Niemeyer

Year

1957

Location
Altonaer Strasse
Berlin 10557
Germany

roombergs.de

In 1953 an urban planning competition was announced to rebuild the Hansaviertel district on the edge of the Tiergarten in West Berlin, which had been heavily bombed during the Second World War. This international housing exposition, known as Interbau, was held in the summer of 1957 to present a model of the 'city of tomorrow' in the International Style and demonstrate the new democratic West Germany to the outside world.

Fifty-three internationally renowned architects were chosen to design buildings for the Hansaviertel neighbourhood, including Oscar Niemeyer from Brazil, Arne Jacobsen from Denmark, Alvar Aalto from Finland and the German Bauhaus founder Walter Gropius. The homes were initially intended as social housing. Alongside residential buildings, two churches, shops, restaurants, a theatre, a library, a kindergarten, an Academy of Arts building by Werner Düttmann and the U-Bahn station at Hansaplatz were also incorporated across the 45-acre site.

The seven-storey building designed by Niemeyer, who was at that time already firmly established as one of Brazil's leading modernist architects, lies in the southwest corner of the Hansaviertel quarter and is surrounded by greenery. The imposing structure stands at 27 metres high and 70 metres long and comprises a concrete frame raised 2 metres off the ground on seven large V-shaped pilotis. A separate triangular elevator tower stands next to the main building, connected to it via bridges on the fifth and seventh floors. The 78 light-filled apartments have generous floor plans ranging from 38 to 91 square metres in size.

A fully restored two-bedroom apartment is available to rent for a minimum of one month, having been refurbished in 2012 by its architect owners. Besides the modern additions of a fully fitted kitchen and two bathrooms, it has been sensitively furnished with mid-century pieces by Egon Eiermann, Harry Bertoia and Eero Saarinen. It accommodates up to four people.

Bauhaus Dessau

Architect
Walter Gropius

Year
1925–26

Location
38 Gropiusallee
Dessau-Rosslau 06846
Germany

bauhaus-dessau.de

Staying at the Bauhaus, considered the birthplace of modernism, is perhaps the ultimate experience of sleeping in a modernist icon. Walter Gropius founded the Bauhaus school in Weimar, Thuringia, in 1919 and relocated it to Dessau in 1926, with a focus on merging teaching, theory and practice. The move allowed Gropius to realise a purpose-designed campus where learning, research, production, partying and eating could all happen under one roof. The expansive building included a student dormitory called the Prellerhaus, an entertainment area with an auditorium, a workshop wing, a wing for the local vocational college and a connecting two-storey bridge, which housed, among other rooms, Gropius's office.

The focus of Bauhaus education was practical training in the workshops, and these rooms remain the most impressive. The reinforced concrete frame, which extends over four floors, allowed for a complete glass facade. The Prellerhaus was placed furthest away from the teaching building. It comprises 28 rooms, each measuring 20 square metres and with a small cantilevered balcony. Initially the bathrooms were located in the basement, but today modern shower rooms are positioned on each floor.

The building was only open for seven years before it was shut down by the Nazis in 1933. Subsequently, several structural modifications were made, including the addition of a shallow pitched roof. During the war, a bombing raid further destroyed it, damaging much of the workshop wing. Despite the odds, it survived and was eventually listed as a historic moment in the 1960s. Several renovation programmes took place over the following years, and today the building is presented just as it would have been originally. Guests can also experience lunch in the authentic canteen or meals in the restaurant and bar in the basement below the Bauhaus workshops.

Masters'
Houses

and

Törten Estate

Architect

Walter
Gropius

Year

1925–28

Locations
57 Ebertallee
Dessau-Rosslau 06846
Germany

Siedlung Dessau-Törten
9 Kleinring
Dessau-Rosslau 06849
Germany

bauhaus-dessau.de

Constructed in 1925–26 and designed by Walter Gropius, the Masters' Houses are a colony of three pairs of identical semi-detached houses (pictured above) built for the Bauhaus teachers, along with a detached house for Gropius, the school's director, all located in pine woods a ten-minute walk from the Bauhaus building. The uniform white exteriors sit in contrast with the colourful designs of the interior spaces, which were chosen by the Masters themselves. After the closure of the school, the city of Dessau rented out the houses and several modifications were made, making them almost unrecognisable. Two of the homes, including Gropius's house, were utterly destroyed by air raids during the war. The remaining houses, however, have undergone a faithful restoration, and in 2014 the Berlin-based architecture practice Bruno Fioretti Marquez replaced the missing buildings with contemporary interpretations. Apart from the Muche/Schlemmer House, all of the buildings are open to the public.

In 1926 the city of Dessau commissioned Gropius to design the Törten Estate, a scheme of affordable housing on the southern edge of the town. This opportunity allowed Gropius to realise one of his ambitions: to create housing using prefabricated components as a means of tackling the housing shortage. On-site mass production of the components, mainly in concrete and breeze-blocks, and a fast pace of construction were employed to keep costs down. The estate was constructed in three phases. The first, in 1926, comprised sixty single-storey houses with gardens, one of which was furnished with products produced in the Bauhaus workshops and was opened to the public during the inauguration of the Bauhaus building. In the second and third phases of construction, Gropius was able to address some of the initial design shortcomings. Guided tours of the entire estate are offered in several languages.

Haus Schminke

Architect

Hans Scharoun

Year

1930–33

Location
1B Kirschallee
Löbau 02708
Germany

stiftung-hausschminke.eu

Haus Schminke, in Löbau, eastern Germany, offers visitors the rare opportunity to experience one of the world's most significant modernist houses first hand, with overnight stays available for up to twelve people. It was designed by the architect Hans Scharoun in 1930 for the successful industrialist Fritz Schminke, who owned a pasta factory nearby.

The design of the house marks a critical stage in the 'organic modernism' movement. Schminke's brief to the architect was straightforward: he wanted 'A modern home for two parents, four children and occasionally one or two guests'. Unlike the formal language of some of his contemporaries, Scharoun's design responded directly to the site. The sloping terrain, with magnificent views to the northeast and of Schminke's factory to the south, proved a challenging location. Wanting to maximise the view and light, Scharoun placed the main body of the house facing south but turned the east and west ends at a 26-degree angle. Extensive glazing eliminates the barriers between the inside and the outside.

The width of the building is approximately 5 metres; on the east side is the living room, with a fully glazed winter garden and terrace, beneath which the ground falls away dramatically. There is a further patio on the first floor, linked to the lower level by an external staircase and covered with a cantilevered roof. Scharoun's fascination with ships influenced the house's distinctive shape. Colour is used in a carefully orchestrated manner, such as the expressive red bullseye in the eastern side of the playroom, the red and white bannisters, the red timber window frames and the yellow brick chimney.

In 1978 Haus Schminke became a protected listed building although in desperate need of maintenance, and finally in 1996 it received funding for conservation and repair, with the work completed in 2000. Guided tours are also available.

Haus des Volkes

Architect
Alfred Arndt

Year
1925–27

Location
25 Bahnhofstrasse
Probstzella 07330
Germany

bauhaushotel.com

With its central turret and pitched roof, on first impression the Haus des Volkes (House of the People) seems an unlikely candidate as one of the largest Bauhaus ensembles in the Thuringia region. Situated in the small town of Probstzella in the mountainous Thuringian Forest, the building was the brainchild of idealistic local entrepreneur and social democrat Franz Itting. Itting had the ambitious vision to create a cultural and recreational centre for his home town that would include a cinema, a dance and theatre hall, a library, a bowling alley, a sauna, a park with a kiosk and a gym.

Itting's son, Gotthardt, studied at the Bauhaus and introduced his father to Bauhaus Master Alfred Arndt and his wife, the photographer Gertrud Arndt. Planning for a traditional-looking building had already been approved before Itting gave the project over to Alfred Arndt, so the Bauhaus architect had to work within the constraints of the existing exterior design. Internally, however, he had a free hand, and this is evident in the colourful staircases and Bauhaus wayfinding typography throughout the building. The Haus des Volkes is one of the few realised examples of complete interior fittings by the Bauhaus workshop. Additional buildings, including a small brick kiosk clad in brass, a flat-roofed café pavilion with glazing wrapping around it, and a concert shell designed by Arndt, were added.

After the Second World War the Haus des Volkes was used for various purposes and suffered unsympathetic alterations, including the lowering and covering of the original roof and skylights in the main hall. In 2003 a local couple who wanted to continue the original ideals of Itting bought and saved the building before its complete decay and set about faithfully restoring it, preserving the original fittings or replacing them based on archival research. In 2005 this unusual building reopened as the Bauhaus Hotel, attracting both architecture fans and mountain hikers.

Werkbund-siedlung Neubühl

Architects
Collective

Year
1932

Location
79 Nidelbadstrasse
Zurich 8038
Switzerland

swb-gästewohnung-neubühl.ch

Following the first Werkbund housing exhibition in Stuttgart in 1927, several similar schemes followed in Brno, Breslau (now Wrocław), Prague, Vienna and Zurich, unified by their architectural appearance of simplified facades. The Werkbundsiedlung Neubühl in Zurich was the largest of all the Werkbund developments and was conceived as a non-profit housing cooperative by a group of young architects comprising Max Ernst Haefeli, Carl Hubacher, Rudolf Steiger, Werner M. Moser, Emil Roth, Paul Artaria and Hans Schmidt. The architects acquired an attractive plot of land in Wollishofen, a southern district of Zurich, and worked collaboratively on the project.

The houses are arranged in rows perpendicular to the streets, making the most of the sun and light and the views of Lake Zurich. Great emphasis was placed on the landscaping, which was designed by the well-known Swiss landscape architect Gustav Ammann. The scheme was completed in 1932 and comprised 195 units in a wide variety of types: 105 two- and three-storey houses, and 90 apartments ranging from one- to six-room units. There were also four retail units, a primary school, and apartments that could be rented out to friends and family. Several restorations have taken place over the years, including in 1986, which saw the sensitive upgrading of bathrooms and kitchens.

Since 2015 one of the studio apartments, accommodating up to two people, has been available to rent as a holiday home. It is looked after and managed immaculately by SWB (the Swiss Werkbund), who have equipped it with furniture of the time, such as day beds designed by Alfred Roth, lounge chairs by Werner M. Moser and stools by Max Bill. It retains many original features, including built-in wardrobes and elegant door furniture. For anyone interested in the architecture and history of the Werkbund housing programmes, a stay in the apartment offers a unique experience.

Villa "Le Lac"
Le Corbusier

Architects

Le Corbusier

and

Pierre Jeanneret

Year

1923–24

Location
21 Route de Lavaux
Corseaux 1802
Switzerland

villalelac.ch

In 1919, Le Corbusier's parents sold their home in La Chaux-de-Fonds, Switzerland. Known as the Maison Blanche (today open to the public), it had been designed for them by their son only seven years earlier, but the couple needed a smaller house to live in during their retirement years, and as they could not afford domestic help they wanted something functional and easy to maintain.

Alongside his partner Pierre Jeanneret, Le Corbusier settled on a secluded spot on the eastern shoreline of Lake Geneva in the Swiss municipality of Corseaux. Villa "Le Lac" is a modest single-storey house measuring only 64 square metres. It is oriented to the south to make the most of the views of the lake and the Alps, with a single 11-metre-long ribbon window running the length of the main living space. Inside, the long, narrow house is open plan and divided into zones, with movable partition walls to subdivide the guest quarters. Sections of the walls are painted in bright colours. At one end of the plot is the garden — or the 'green hall', as Le Corbusier called it — with a white stone wall and a square window framing the landscape. In the Villa "Le Lac", Le Corbusier achieved three of the principles of his Five Points of a New Architecture: a roof garden, a free plan and a horizontal window.

The house was completed in 1924 and his parents moved in shortly afterwards, with his mother living there until her death at the grand age of one hundred. The building suffered a series of structural problems and over the years many remedial works and interventions were carried out, including the cladding of the north facade with galvanised steel in 1931, and the south facade with aluminium in 1951. More recently both the exterior and the garden were restored. This 'minimal house' marked an important milestone in Le Corbusier's thinking and influenced many of his subsequent projects. Now run by the Association Villa "Le Lac" Le Corbusier, the house is open to the public.

Bauhaus Hotel Monte Verità

Architect
Emil Fahrenkamp

Year
1927–29

Location
84 Strada Collina
Ascona 6612
Switzerland

monteverita.org

In the autumn of 1900, a group of six young people travelled around northern Italy and southern Switzerland seeking an alternative life, away from capitalism. They had an ambitious plan to buy a piece of land on which to build a new commune based around nature, health, purity and truth. They settled on a small wine-growing mountain near Ascona in Ticino and named it Monte Verità (Mountain of Truth). Working long hours, they planted vegetable gardens and built huts made of timber, stone and lime. To finance the project they welcomed paying guests, and soon the health benefits of this new sanatorium gained a reputation among artists, philosophers and intellectuals. Purification rituals included a strict vegetarian diet, sunbathing and dancing.

When in 1920 the founders emigrated to Brazil the commune disbanded, and Baron von der Heydt, a banker and prominent art collector, bought the whole complex and gave it a new lease of life. In 1927 he commissioned the leading German architect and professor Emil Fahrenkamp to design a new hotel, now called the Bauhaus Hotel.

Built against the rock face, the building's exterior and interior design is in the Bauhaus tradition, with a white facade and large windows on the first floor opening to a long balcony. On the upper floors, the facade is set back to provide space for a two-storey loggia accessed from the bedrooms. Thanks to the new hotel, Monte Verità was visited by Bauhaus masters such as Walter Gropius, Josef Albers, Herbert Bayer, Marcel Breuer and László Moholy-Nagy. Ise Gropius described it in 1978 as a 'place where our minds can reach up to the heavens'.

Today Monte Verità is a state-of-the-art congress and cultural centre. The building was recently restored and boasts original features, Bauhaus furnishings as well as rooms with spectacular views of the lake. In 2013 it received the Historic Hotel of the Year Award from the International Council on Monuments and Sites.

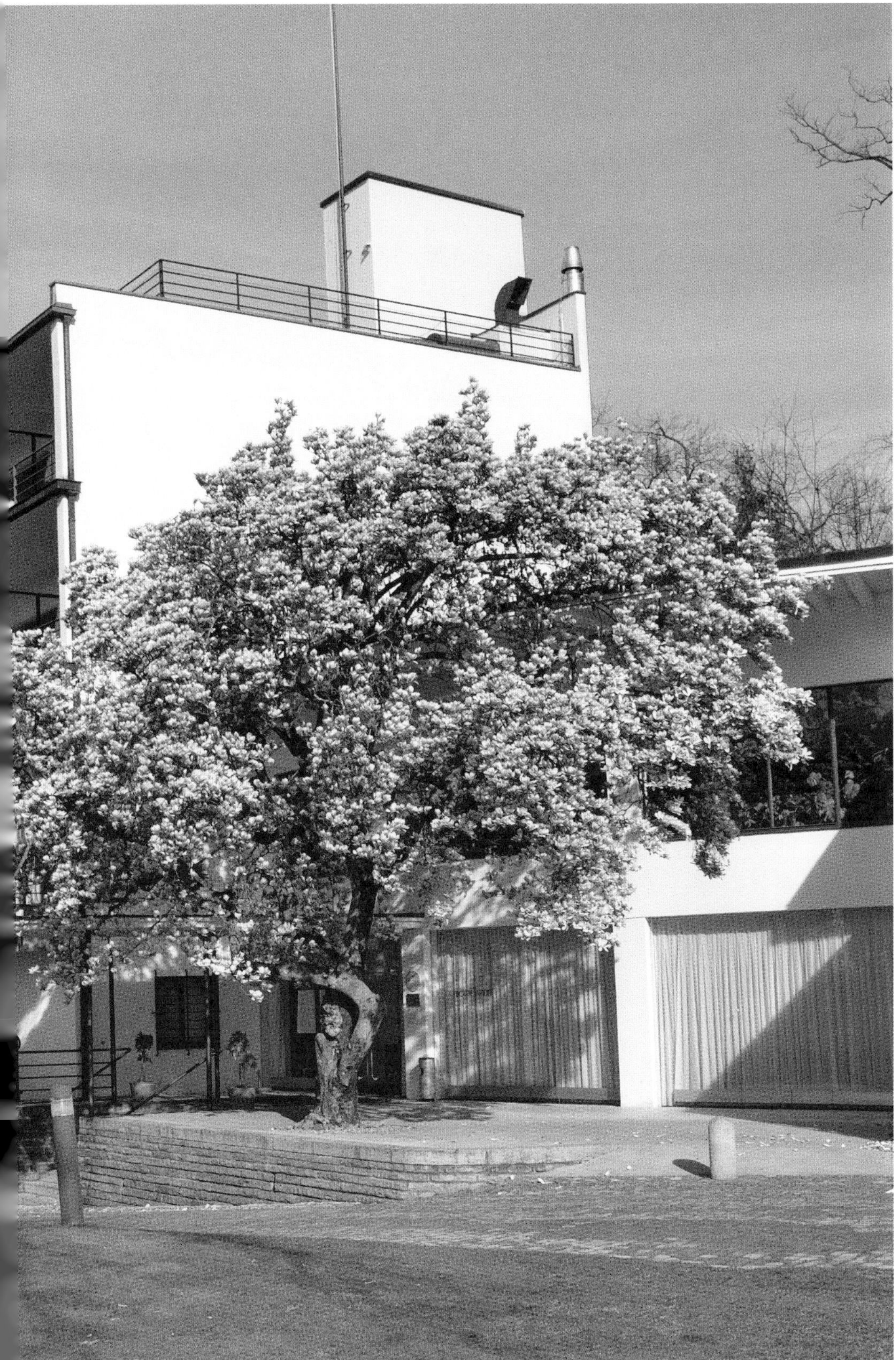

House Dellacher

Architect
Raimund Abraham

Year
1965–69

Location
169 Grazerstrasse
Oberwart 7400
Austria

dasdellacher.at

Built between 1965 and 1969 and situated on a hillside by the edge of a forest in Austria's easternmost Burgenland region, House Dellacher was designed by the Austrian-born architect Raimund Abraham for his childhood friend Max Dellacher, a photographer, and his wife. Abraham, perhaps best known for the Austrian Cultural Forum tower in New York, shared a vision with Dellacher of what a modern house could be, and the two men worked closely together on the design. In 1964, before construction began, Abraham left Austria and relocated to the US, but he continued to work on the commission by sending sketches and drawings to Austria, and these were drawn up into blueprints by the architect Rudolf Schober.

With arcades and a white facade, the design broadly follows the traditional regional style, although Abraham denied that intention. The commanding shape of the exterior breaks away from the modern architectural style of the time, being characterised by its symmetrical staircases, reminiscent of Italian Renaissance villas, with a swimming pool placed in front. The interior is dominated by a spiral staircase illuminated by a skylight. Built-in furniture not dissimilar to the work of Adolf Loos is incorporated into wood-panelled niches.

After the death of Dellacher the house became the property of a bank and remained empty and in urgent need of extensive renovation. It became a listed building in 2006, and finally, in 2015, it was rescued by the architect Johannes Handler, who meticulously restored it to its former glory and saved its original features, including the hardwood floors, built-in furniture, lighting and even the light switches. To guarantee the future of this internationally significant building, the Das Dellacher Association was formed and the house opened its doors to the public, offering regular guided tours.

Looshaus Hotel and Restaurant

Architect
Adolf Loos

Year
1930

Location
60 Kreuzberg
Payerbach 2650
Austria

looshaus.at

'Do not be afraid of being called unfashionable. Changes in old methods are only allowed when they are an improvement, otherwise, stick with the old', wrote Adolf Loos — which may go some way to explain how, only two years after completing the modernist Villa Müller in Prague (see page 239), this alpine house on the slopes of Semmering at first appears to be designed by a completely different architect.

The house was built in 1930 for Paul Khuner, a successful food manufacturer who wanted a home for himself, his wife and their three daughters and additional bedrooms for guests. In the Khuner House, Loos chose to use the language and materials of the traditional alpine lodge, such as timber cladding and large pitched roof. The building sits on a wide base of local stone, overlooking the mountain landscape.

Once inside the house, Loos's distinctive Raumplan — a term he coined to describe the arrangement of rooms revolving around stairs — is immediately apparent: a small oak-beamed hall offers a confusing number of options for which way to go. Enter into the living room and you are confronted with a spectacularly large, bright double-height space, with one wall of glazing framing dramatic views of the mountain meadows. On the first floor, the main bedrooms are organised around a gallery that wraps around three walls. Each room has a lively colour theme, oak panelling and beds built into alcoves — a signature of Loos's mature work.

The Khuners left the house in the late 1930s, and in 1959 it was transformed into the Looshaus Hotel and Restaurant by the Steiner family, who are still at the helm today, welcoming both mountain walkers and architecture enthusiasts. Aside from the addition of bathrooms, the rooms have been very well preserved — purists will not be disappointed.

Brummel House

Architect
Adolf Loos

Year
1929

Location
58 Husova
Pilsen 301 00
Czech Republic

adolfloosplzen.cz

Alongside individual houses, Adolf Loos designed several interiors, particularly in the Czech town of Pilsen, situated 90 kilometres west of Prague. His clients were predominantly wealthy Jewish families. Eight of these interiors have survived and have been restored, and six of those are open to the public for guided tours, including the impressive Brummel House, which was Austrian-born Loos's first commission in Pilsen. It was designed in 1927 and completed in 1929 for Hans (or Jan) Brummel, his wife Hanni (Jana) and her mother, Hedvika Liebstein. Working with architect Karel Lhota, Loos designed a two-storey extension to the original house, which was owned by Mrs Liebstein, who had the lifelong right to live there. Access to the apartment is via a staircase, the architectural design of which, at the request of the client, is a copy of the classicist Goethe House, designed by the architect Georg Caspar Helmershausen in Weimar, Germany.

The apartment features a well-thought-out interior layout, with sophisticated combinations of materials and coloured surface finishes as well as surprising elements such as a huge Provence Renaissance fireplace (again a request of the client) in the living room. In the bedroom, Loos defined individual functions by using varying ceiling heights; while the dining room's light-coloured Canadian poplar panelling is complemented with green wallpaper, green felt on the floor and oriental rugs. Mrs Liebstein's colourful salon, used for working and socialising, and her bedroom, panelled in maple wood with a band of green wallpaper above it, demonstrate characteristics typical of Loos's designs.

During the Nazi German occupation the Brummels were forced out of the house and sent to concentration camps. Although they survived, the house then became the property of the state during the Czechoslovakian communist era. During restitution, ownership of the house was returned to the family, and in 2001 it was immaculately restored.

Villa Müller

Architect
Adolf Loos

Year
1928–30

Location
14/642 Nad Hradním
vodojemem
Střešovice
Prague 162 00
Czech Republic

muzeumprahy.cz/
mullerova-vila

The affluent civil engineer and building contractor František Müller commissioned Adolf Loos, assisted by Karel Lhota, to design a house for his family in 1928. Completed two years later, the Villa Müller is one of the finest examples of modernist architecture and of Loos's Raumplan, a term he coined to describe his approach to the arrangement of spaces: 'I do not design plans, facades or sections, I design spaces. For me there is no ground floor, first floor and so on … For me there are only contiguous spaces … the storeys merge and the spaces relate to each other.'

As in the Villa Winternitz (see page 240) the space is dominated by the living room, which spans two levels, linking through to the dining room, the study and Milada Müller's boudoir. On the higher levels are the children's bedrooms and the cloakrooms. At the very top is an impressive Japanese-inspired salon, used as a summer dining room. The villa's opulent interior is characterised by a rich colour palette, extensive use of marble and wood cladding, and luxurious furniture. In stark contrast, the exterior is painted a crisp white, with no decoration except for the bright yellow irregularly placed window frames.

As non-Jewish Czechs, the Müllers managed to live in the villa throughout the Second World War. The situation changed drastically, however, when the communists came to power in 1948. The house was seized, and although the Müllers were allowed to stay there, their accommodation was limited to only two rooms. František Müller died a few years later, and Milada lived there until her death in 1968. The Velvet Revolution of 1989 saw the house transferred back to the family, who subsequently sold it to the city of Prague. After extensive reconstruction and restoration of its surviving original interior fittings, the villa was opened to the public in 2000 and now offers regular guided tours.

Villa Winternitz

Architects

Adolf Loos

and

Karel Lhota

Year

1931–32

Location
10 Na Cihlářce
Prague 150 00
Czech Republic

loosovavila.cz

The Villa Winternitz was one of the last projects Adolf Loos completed in his lifetime. It was designed in 1931 in collaboration with Karel Lhota for the lawyer Josef Winternitz and his family. The arrangement of the space follows Loos's Raumplan concept and bears a resemblance to his Villa Müller (see page 239), albeit on a smaller budget. A grand two-level living room occupies the entire width of the building and is entered via large glazed doors from a terrace. A wooden staircase leads up to the raised level, which is divided by two pillars delineating the dining and the sitting area. The bedrooms are located on the upper floors.

The Winternitzes lived in the house until 1941, when they were forced out under racial persecution, and it was transferred to the Central Office for Jewish Emigration in Prague. It was subsequently sold to the city of Prague, who turned the villa into a kindergarten. Tragically, the Winternitz family were deported in 1943 and sent to Auschwitz, where Josef and his son, Peter, were murdered. Josef's wife, Jenny, and daughter, Suzana, survived and returned to Prague after liberation. The Czech state recognised their entitlement to the house, but under the law at that time they were required to pay inheritance and luxury tax. Unable to afford such sums, they had little choice but to donate the villa back to the Czechoslovak government. They never saw or spoke of the house again.

It was not until the restitution of 1991 that the rest of the family found out about the villa. By this time, however, both Suzana and her mother had died. Josef's grandson Stanislav Cysař decided to fund its restoration—fortunately, much of its original fixtures, such as built-in furniture, cabinets, mirrors and shelves, had survived. Today it is open to the public during the day and offers the unique opportunity for two guests to experience the villa at night, when at 6 p.m. the staff hand over the keys to the entire building until 10 a.m. the next day.

AXA Hotel

Architect

Václav Pilc

Year

1930–32

Location
40 Na Poříčí
Prague 110 00
Czech Republic

axa-hotel.cz

The functionalist AXA Hotel, completed in 1932 in the centre of Prague, was conceived by architect and master builder Václav Pilc and his wife, Běla Friedländer, a successful sportswoman who represented the First Czechoslovak Republic in swimming and diving. The couple had the ambitious idea of running a modern sports-oriented hotel with a 25-metre swimming pool and two gyms, where Friedländer would hold sports classes mainly intended for girls and women. The technically advanced building included central heating, air conditioning and a dust-removal system across the hotel as well as incorporating commercial spaces, shops, restaurants and offices. The hotel rooms were furnished mainly with tubular furniture from Slezákovy Závody, one of the largest producers of metal furniture in Czechoslovakia.

The couple ran the hotel until 1948, when it was nationalised, after which it underwent several alterations, the most significant being between 1978 and 1985 when the pool was modified, with the diving board removed and the depth reduced. In 1994 the ownership of the hotel was transferred back to the family, and a decade later they undertook the major restoration of the building, modernising it to meet today's standards while still evoking the original 1930s spirit. Anything that was intact or could be repaired was preserved, while replicas based on the original designs furnish the bedrooms. The original colours of beige, red and blue have also been reinstated. The AXA Hotel opened its doors again in 2015, including the public swimming pool and fitness centre. A year later it was designated a cultural monument by the Czech Ministry of Culture as an example of the poetic functionalist style.

Villa Tugendhat

Architect

Ludwig Mies van der Rohe

Year

1928–30

Location
45 Černopolní
Brno 613 00
Czech Republic

tugendhat.eu

Combining luxury and classical nobility, Villa Tugendhat in Brno is an outstanding example of a residential house in the International Style. It was designed by German-born architect Ludwig Mies van der Rohe between 1928 and 1929 for the Jewish newlyweds Greta and Fritz Tugendhat. Greta's father, Alfred Löw-Beer, an industrialist, gave a plot of land to his daughter on a location just behind his own house, Villa Löw-Beer (also open to the public).

The modern couple's brief to Mies van der Rohe was for a house with 'lightness, airiness and clarity'. Impressed by the location — a south-facing slope with views towards the landscape and city of Brno — the architect agreed to take on the commission at a time when he was also working on the Barcelona Pavilion for the 1929 Universal Exposition. The Villa Tugendhat was the first private house in history to use load-bearing steel columns — here in the form of a chrome-faced cruciforms. The architect also designed the furniture and the adjacent garden. Trusting the architect's vision, the Tugendhats did not impose any financial constraints, and expensive materials such as onyx from Morocco, ebony, Italian travertine and Southeast Asian woods were used along with novel construction methods. State-of-the-art technologies for heating and cooling systems were also incorporated. Although the overall cost is not known, reportedly it was the equivalent of thirty small family homes.

In 1938, eight years after the villa's completion and a year before the Nazi takeover of Czechoslovakia, the Tugendhats fled to Switzerland. The building was subsequently taken over by the Gestapo and much of the interior demolished. After numerous inhabitants and uses, including as a stables for a Russian cavalry unit, it became almost unrecognisable, but despite this it was declared a cultural monument in 1995. It underwent an ambitious restoration programme and is now open to the public with well-informed guided tours in several languages.

Melnikov House

Architect
Konstantin Melnikov

Year
1927–29

Location
10 Krivoarbatsky Lane
Moscow 119002
Russia

muar.ru

The highly original Melnikov House, designed between 1927 and 1929 in Moscow, does not easily fall into a specific architectural movement. The Russian architect and painter Konstantin Melnikov designed the building for his personal use as a family home and studio, and its design took inspiration from American silos and Russian churches. The house is situated on a residential street in the city centre, on a small plot of land granted to him in order to build an experimental prototype building using innovative construction techniques that could be rolled out in mass housing.

This avant-garde structure comprises two intersecting cylindrical volumes, each measuring 9 metres in diameter—one is 8 metres high and the other 11 metres. The cylinders are perforated with a grid of sixty hexagonal windows. The brick exteriors function as the load-bearing walls, eliminating the need for columns and thus creating uninterrupted, enigmatic interiors. The shorter of the two volumes faces the street and is dominated by glass curtain walling that runs the full height of the building. Basic materials such as brick, wood and plaster were used to minimise construction costs.

On the ground floor, the architect placed the dining room, kitchen, bathroom and children's workrooms. On the first floor, reached by a straight staircase, is a spacious double-height living room with full-height windows in one cylinder, and an open-plan space for the parents' and children's bedrooms (initially separated by two partitions) in the other. A spiral staircase links the living room to the double-height studio and terrace. The walls are painted in a palette of muted tones.

Sadly, Melnikov's career was cut short when in 1936 he was exiled from practising his profession. He lived in the Melnikov House until his death in 1974, following which, according to the wishes of the architect's son, the artist Viktor Melnikov, the building was restored, and it is now open as a house museum.

Oskar Hansen House

Architects

Oskar and Zofia Hansen

Year

1968

Location
4 Mlekicie
Szumin 07-130
Poland

artmuseum.pl

The Hansen House is not your typical house museum where furniture is carefully positioned with the occasional 'Please Do Not Touch' sign. Designed by Polish architect, artist and theorist Oskar Hansen and his wife, Zofia Hansen, as a summer residence for their family, the home in Szumin was designed to act as the backdrop to the richness of daily life, and the presence of its former inhabitants can still be felt.

Oskar Hansen was born in Helsinki in 1922 and after the Second World War studied at Warsaw University of Technology's faculty of architecture. From 1948 to 1950 he visited France, Italy and England and studied under Fernand Léger and Le Corbusier's cousin Pierre Jeanneret. He later became a member of Team 10, a group of architects that rejected the modernist doctrine 'a house is a machine for living in', and at a CIAM congress he openly criticised Le Corbusier. Ten years later, at another CIAM meeting, Hansen promoted his Open Form theory. The concept aimed to engage the viewer, recipient and user by creating adaptive architectural frames that could be filled by the everyday events of its users.

His summer house is the most significant spatial manifesto of Open Form. It was constructed in several stages from 1968, jointly by Oskar, Zofia and their son Igor. The unobtrusive wooden structure with a characteristic pitched roof is located in the picturesque area of an oxbow bend of the Bug River in Mazovia. The house was designed to connect with the landscape, engaging the senses and blurring the distinction between interior and exterior. Since 2014 the Museum of Modern Art in Warsaw has been its custodian, and with the presence of visitors, the house comes to life following the Open Form principles, just as Hansen intended.

Villa Tammekann

Architect

Alvar Aalto

Year

1932

Location
6 Friedrich Reinhold
Kreutzwaldi
Tartu 51006
Estonia

villatammekann.fi

The Villa Tammekann in Tartu is the only building in Estonia designed by Finnish architect Alvar Aalto. It was commissioned in 1932 by Professor August Tammekann, who wanted a small family house. Due to the Great Depression, however, sourcing the building materials specified by Aalto was difficult and resulted in several significant compromises to the design. The walls, for example, had to be made 25 centimetres thicker for insulation, making the corridors substantially narrower. The Tammerkanns moved into the three-storey house in 1933, although it was still unfinished.

The Second World War altered the fate of Estonia as well as that of the Tammekann family. They fled the Soviet occupation in the summer of 1940 and following the war the Villa Tammekann was nationalised. Subsequently, it was divided into separate small apartments for up to eight households, and the flat roof was replaced with a pitched alternative.

In 1991, during the Soviet military coup attempt in Moscow, Estonia declared the restoration of its independence, reconstituting the pre-1940 state. This also freed the villa from Soviet control, and in 1994 it was returned to its original owners. A few years later it was bought by the Turku University Foundation, who in collaboration with the Aalto Foundation restored it to its original design. The flat roof was rebuilt and the garage and pergola, central to Aalto's original concept, were finally built. The internal dividing walls that had been erected after the war were torn down, and the spaces of the ground and first floors were returned almost to their original appearance and furnished with furniture by Artek, the firm co-founded by Aalto in 1935.

It is now home to the Granö Centre of the universities of Tartu and Turku, who offer tours of the house as well as overnight accommodation, primarily intended for university staff but also open to special groups interested in Aalto's architecture.

Radisson Collection Royal Hotel

Architect

Arne Jacobsen

Year

1961

Location
1 Hammerichsgade
Copenhagen 1611
Denmark

radissonhotels.com

This 22-storey hotel near the Tivoli Gardens in the centre of Copenhagen stands as a temple to the spirit of the 1960s jet age. Originally named the SAS Royal, it was designed by Arne Jacobsen for the Scandinavian airline SAS, who had the futuristic idea of a hotel that would double up as an airport terminal. A shuttle bus, also designed by Jacobsen, transported well-heeled travellers directly from its elegant cocktail lounge to Kastrup Airport in twenty minutes.

The building comprises two rectangular volumes: at the base is a horizontal block, with another block placed on top, running vertically. As the first skyscraper in Copenhagen, the proposed building caused controversy at the time, but Jacobsen was sensitive to the fact that it would sit among mainly low-rise buildings and carefully chose materials to ensure it would not be overly dominant. He used a reinforced concrete construction with a glass curtain wall, utilising materials and colours that had a sense of lightness, such as the grey-green glass on the facade, which gently reflects the shifting colours of the sky.

Everything from the carpets, curtains, door handles and lamps to the cutlery, ashtrays and hotel signage was designed by Jacobsen. A number of his best-known designs, such as the Swan and Egg chairs, were initially created for the SAS Royal. Unfortunately, only a few years after it opened in 1961, several alterations and refurbishments were made, until eventually the hotel was almost unrecognisable except for Room 606 (pictured above), which even today remains as the architect created it. In 2018, after a two-year makeover, the 261-room hotel underwent a complete overhaul, preserving and restoring its original character while modernising it and bringing it to life for a new generation.

Finn Juhl House

Architect

Finn Juhl

Year

1942

Location
15 Kratvænget
Charlottenlund 2920
Denmark

ordrupgaard.dk

Along with Arne Jacobsen and Hans Wegner, Finn Juhl was a key figure in mid-century Danish modernism. Although he is best known for his furniture designs, characterised by their sculptural, expressive forms, such as the classic FJ45 armchair, he studied architecture at the Royal Academy in Copenhagen — as a furniture designer, he was mainly self-taught.

Juhl designed and built only a handful of houses in his lifetime, including his own home in 1942 at the edge of a quiet forest in Charlottenlund, 11 kilometres north of Copenhagen. The L-shaped bungalow, built of brick with a grey-white render, is modest and unassuming from the outside. By concentrating on the interiors, Juhl designed the house from the inside out. It comprises two pitched-roof buildings joined by a low entrance hall. One building houses the kitchen, dining room, bedrooms and bathrooms; the other the living room and a small study. The house demonstrates an early example of open-plan living, with a natural sense of flow from one space to another but each having a distinct function. Large windows offer views of the garden from every room.

In contrast with the facade, the interior is a delightful array of materials, textures and colours. A bright blue entrance hall gives way to the more muted tones of the rest of the house. A painted yellow ceiling reflects the light, helping to bring the outside in, with Juhl's collection of arts and crafts — including furnishings of his own design, some of which are unique to the house — scattered throughout the home. The architect-designer lived here until his death in 1989, and twenty years later it was fully restored and it is now managed and preserved by the Ordrupgaard museum, offering regular guided tours in several languages.

Villa Stenersen

Architect
Arne Korsmo

Year
1937–39

Location
10C Tuengen Allé
Oslo 0374
Norway

nasjonalmuseet.no

A couple of years after graduating in 1926 as an architect from the Norwegian Institute of Technology in Trondheim, Arne Korsmo travelled to mainland Europe on an architectural tour. He returned to Oslo full of new ideas about modern architecture and began his practice, becoming one of the leading figures of the International Style in Norway.

His approach towards architecture was to combine the logical with the poetic, and the Villa Stenersen, designed in 1937–39 and regarded as one of his major works, is an excellent example of his aims. The house, situated on a slope overlooking a fjord coastline in Oslo, was designed for the businessman and art collector Rolf Stenersen and his family.

The four-storey building is split into three horizontal sections, each level differentiated by colour and material, indicating a different function for each floor. One enters through a curved vestibule that mimics the curved wall of the drive-through garage. A garden room on the ground floor with an illustrated decorated column and a curved fireplace welcomes guests. The entire south wall is made of glass. Upstairs, Korsmo designed an open-plan living and dining space to display Stenersen's vast collection of Edvard Munch paintings; the south wall is composed wholly of glass blocks, diffusing light into the room. A large and sculptural terrazzo staircase is situated at the north side of the house, its walls also intended to display the art collection, lit by a stunning perforated skylight made from 625 circular glass cylinders in three different blues. On the top floor, facing west, is the master bedroom, and further bedrooms run along the south of the plan.

In 1974 Stenersen donated his family home to the Norwegian state, and in the spring of 2014 the National Museum of Art, Architecture and Design took over its administration. The house now opens to the public from May to October, with regular tours.

Villa Mairea

Architect

Alvar Aalto

Year

1938–39

Location
20 Pikkukoivukuja
Noormarkku 29600
Finland

villamairea.fi

Villa Mairea is one of Alvar Aalto's most important works. It was designed for his friends and clients Maire (née Ahlström) and Harry Gullichsen. Maire, an art patron and artist, was the granddaughter of Antti Ahlström, founder of the A. Ahlström corporation, and Harry Gullichsen the firm's CEO. In 1935, along with Alvar and Aino Aalto and the art historian and critic Nils-Gustaf Hahl, the Gullichsens established Finnish furniture company Artek.

A few years later the Gullichsens commissioned Aalto to design them a large family summer house on the Ahlström estate in Noormarkku in western Finland. The estate was already home to two houses belonging to Ahlström directors. As supporters of modern art and architecture, the Gullichsens wanted a house that would represent a vision of modern life. The clients approved the plans in 1938; however, at a late stage — when excavations for the foundations had already begun — Aalto, unsatisfied with the design, decided to modify it. The initial design included a basement and a separate room for the couple's art collection, but in the revised plans these were done away with — resulting in a 250-square-metre living space broken up by rhythmically placed vertical columns and poles on the ground floor, and a private living space and painting studio upstairs. The art collection was instead integrated into the everyday environment of the house and can be viewed today as part of the house guided tour.

Set on a hilltop with views across the forest, from a distance the Villa Mairea, with its white box exterior, could pass for an orthodox modernist house. However, inside, Aalto's playful use of natural forms, colours and textures, fluid lines and organic materials — including the forest-like space of the living room — makes clear his move away from the dogmatic face of modernism. Villa Mairea is today partly in private use, and visits are possible with prior reservation.

Muuratsalo Experimental House

Architect
Alvar Aalto

Year
1952–54

Location
2 Melalammentie
Jyväskylä 40900
Finland

alvaraalto.fi

The Experimental House is situated on the western shore of Muuratsalo island, in the waters of Lake Päijänne in southern Finland. The unspoilt site was discovered by Alvar Aalto and his second wife, Elissa, when they were working together on the town hall for the nearby island of Säynätsalo. The land was owned by the Ahlström company, whose director, Harry Gullichsen, was a close friend and client—Aalto had designed his Villa Mairea in 1938 (see page 264)—and the couple managed to purchase it. In 1952 they designed and built a summer house on the site that also served as a laboratory for their architectural experiments.

The modest house is primarily built of rejected bricks from their Säynätsalo Town Hall project and is formed of two wings: one contains the living room, with an elevated loft space above — which they used as a painting studio—and the other holds two bedrooms, the bathroom and the kitchen. The L-shaped building wraps around an internal courtyard with a firepit at its centre. Two tall, ruin-like walls enclose this central gathering space while offering views south towards the lake and of the pine trees to the west. In 1953 Aalto built an additional wooden guest wing with two bedrooms; there is also a separate sauna building and a woodshed. The project gave Aalto the freedom to test many innovative ideas, including building without foundations and experiments in the weathering and aesthetics of brick. Whereas the facade of the main building is rendered white, the walls around the courtyard are a stunning patchwork of red bricks, arranged in fifty different ways.

Today the Experimental House is in private hands but it can be visited in the summer season as part of a guided tour led by the Alvar Aalto Foundation. Also on display is the unique motorboat Aalto designed for transporting his family to the house when access to it was only possible by water.

Aalto House and Studio

Architect

Alvar Aalto

Year

1935/1955

Location
20 Riihitie and 20 Tiilimäki
Helsinki 00330
Finland

alvaraalto.fi

In 1934 Alvar Aalto and his first wife, Aino, acquired a plot of land in Munkkiniemi, a neighbourhood of Helsinki, where they built a house and studio. The design of the house marked a departure for Aalto from strict functionalism to the softer, more romantic architecture that he would later explore more fully at Villa Mairea (see page 264). As with all of the private houses he designed, mostly for friends, the building is an integration between the living and working environments. The L-shaped volume comprises a double-height studio with a mezzanine in one wing and the private living spaces in the other. These different functions are reflected in the facade of the building—the studio is of whitewashed brick, whereas the bedrooms, located on the second floor of the other wing, are clad in dark-stained timber battens.

In the interior Aalto combined natural materials, such as wooden floors and screens, with simple, clean living spaces and carefully designed furniture. A large sliding screen separates the house's residential area from the studio space, with the bedrooms reached via a central landing that also serves as a breakfast area with a fireplace. The landing gives direct access to the large roof terrace, reminiscent of the Bauhaus Masters' Houses by Walter Gropius in Dessau, Germany (see page 214). In 1955, in response to his architecture practice's gradual growth, Aalto decided to build a larger studio five minutes' walk from the house. This building consists of two drafting rooms each with a reception area, an archive and a conference room. The principal space is an impressive curving studio that opens out to the garden-amphitheatre. Here staff could listen to lectures or watch slide shows projected on the curved white wall.

Aalto lived in the house up until his death in 1976, and it remains largely unchanged. The studio building is now the home of the Alvar Aalto Foundation, and both can be visited as part of a tour.

Villa Skeppet

Architect
Alvar Aalto

Year
1969–70

Location
7 Itäinen Rantakatu
Tammisaari 10600
Finland

villaschildt.fi

The friendship between Alvar Aalto and the writer Göran Schildt began when Schildt visited the architect's office in Helsinki in 1952. In the following years, Schildt published several articles on Aalto's new buildings, and as a token of friendship Aalto offered to design a house for him and his wife. Taking into account the needs and personalities of his clients—primarily, Schildt wanted somewhere peaceful to write, with a connection to nature— Aalto found a suitable plot of land in a park-like setting, off a quiet street in the small coastal town of Tammisaari in the southwest of Finland.

The Villa Skeppet (also known as Villa Schildt), completed in 1970, comprises several buildings. The main house is divided into four areas connected by a narrow hall; to the left of the hall is a large living room, elevated above the garage to give privacy from the street and to make the best of the views. This, along with the projecting wedge-shaped balcony, provides the building with its characterful shape. A sculptural fireplace designed by Aalto takes centre stage in the living room. The more private spaces are to the right of the hallway, including an open-plan kitchen-dining room, while the writer's study is at the end of the hall, overlooking the garden. Joined to the main house by way of a loggia is a separate wing for guests, and a sauna building is positioned parallel to the main house, creating a quiet courtyard garden with a free-form lily pond in the centre. The materials used are typical of Aalto's projects. The lower parts of the building's facade are in white-rendered brick, while the living room is clad in contrastingly dark-stained vertical weatherboarding. Inside, the hall and living rooms are dominated by timber ceilings and monumental beams.

The house is now owned and managed by the Christine and Göran Schildt Foundation; guided tours are available during the summer months by appointment.

Villa Kokkonen

Architect
Alvar Aalto

Year
1967–69

Location
5 Tuulimyllyntie
Järvenpää 04400
Finland

villakokkonen.fi

Since 2009, Villa Kokkonen has been lived in and managed by pianist Elina Viitaila and opera singer Antti A. Pesonen — fitting custodians for a house that was built for one the most well-respected twentieth-century Finnish composers, Joonas Kokkonen. The house was designed in the late 1960s by Kokkonen's friend Alvar Aalto when the architect was 69 years old. His brief was for a building that would function as a place of work as well as a family home. As in all of his residential projects, Aalto placed the individual needs of his client at the centre of the design, and after the two of them visited the site they went to a restaurant, where Aalto made his first sketch — positioning Kokkonen's grand piano at the heart of the plan.

The house is situated on the north side of Lake Tuusula, a 45-minute drive from Helsinki, on a wooded plot that slopes down westward. The existing pine trees were disturbed as little as possible in accommodating the new building, and to blend further with its surroundings it is entirely clad in dark-stained timber. The front facade, facing the street, is modest and inconspicuous. The rear of the building opens out to the garden and nature; additionally, there is a sauna and a pool house. The three primary functions of the house — the living areas, the bedrooms and the kitchen, and the music studio — are clearly defined in the floor plan, but the spaces flow easily from one to another. The studio, which has a double-height ceiling, appears to be part of the house but is in fact structurally wholly separate so that the sound does not permeate the residential parts.

Much of the original furniture, as well as Kokkonen's grand piano and personal collection of artefacts, is preserved and can be viewed during tours of the house, led by the enthusiastic Elina and Antti, who also offer intimate concert performances.

La Ricarda

Architect

Antonio Bonet Castellana

Year

1949–63

Location
El Prat de Llobregat
Barcelona 08820
Spain

Regular organised tours
elprat.cat/turisme-i-territori/
que-visitar/la-casa-gomis

Group tours by appointment
casagomis@laricarda.com

La Ricarda, named after the nearby lake in El Prat de Llobregat, a town southwest of Barcelona, is one of the most culturally significant mid-century houses in Spain. This achievement was the result of three great minds with a shared vision: the architect Antonio Bonet Castellana and his clients Ricardo Gomis and his wife Inés Bertrand. Born in Barcelona, where he studied architecture, Bonet moved to Paris in 1936 to work in Le Corbusier's office, a period that had a profound influence on his work. By the end of 1937 he moved to Argentina, where he gained an international reputation.

In the 1930s the Gomis family had been involved in several avant-garde movements in Spain, mixing in circles with the likes of Joan Miró, Josep Lluís Sert and, crucially, the art promoter Joan Prats. In 1949 the family were looking for the right architect to design them a family house on unspoilt land near the sea and surrounded by pine trees. With Sert in exile, Prats suggested Bonet to them as an alternative. Subsequently Bonet, Gomis and Bertrand formed a great friendship and worked closely together at long-distance, communicating via letters over thirteen years.

The large house, completed in 1963, sits on a raised platform and comprises a series of twelve modules—each with a vaulted ceiling—organised in terms of function. For example, there is a children's module, a parents' module, a dining module and so on. Expansive areas of plate glass throughout the building draw the eye to the outside and the surrounding pine forest garden. Bonet meticulously designed every aspect and detail of the home, from the overall organisation down to the furniture.

During Franco's dictatorship, the family welcomed artists and intellectuals to their home. Today the future of the house is uncertain, threatened by the ever-expanding El Prat Airport. The second generation of the Gomis-Bertrands, however, are working hard to preserve this important and beautiful building.

Casa Bloc

Architects

Josep Lluís Sert, Josep Torres Clavé

and

Joan Baptista Subirana

Year

1933

Location
Carrer de l'Almirall Pròixida
Barcelona 08030
Spain

ajuntament.barcelona.cat

The Casa Bloc apartments in Barcelona's Sant Andreu district — the first social housing project in the city to be built in the functionalist style — were designed in 1933 by Josep Lluís Sert, Josep Torres Clavé and Joan Baptista Subirana, members of GATCPAC (Group of Catalan Architects and Technicians for the Progress of Contemporary Architecture), a group heralding avant-garde Catalan architecture. The apartment blocks were intended to provide decent, affordable homes for local workers, influenced by housing in other major European cities such as Berlin. The original design of the scheme, comprising 207 dwellings, took the form of five seven-storey steel-framed blocks arranged in an S-formation, creating two large open courtyards. The buildings followed Corbusian principles — raised on pilotis with free facades and a free plan. Stairs and lifts provided vertical access, via 'street-in-the-sky' walkways on every other floor, to the duplexes, which ranged from two to four bedrooms. To make the most of the light, the living spaces faced either east or south. Internally, the austere apartments were simple yet functional; although elegant, they avoided any pretension of luxury.

The outbreak of the Spanish Civil War in 1936 brought the apartments' construction to a standstill until 1940. The subsequent Franco dictatorship, however, changed the course of the project. The homes were given to military officers and families, and several compromising alternations were made to the individual buildings and the overall scheme.

The past thirty years have seen a significant restoration project at Casa Bloc and a reversal of much of the damage, both internally and externally. One of the apartments, a two-bedroom duplex, has recently been meticulously restored to its original state, complete with furniture of the period. Guided tours of the apartment give visitors an insight into Casa Bloc and its significance in the story of modern housing prototypes.

Casa Broner

Architect

Erwin Broner

Year

1960

Location
15 Carrer de la Penya
Ibiza 07800
Balearic Islands
Spain

eivissa.es/mace

The modernist home of Erwin Broner sits atop cliffs among the historic buildings of Sa Penya in Ibiza. The son of an affluent Jewish family, Broner initially studied painting in his native country of Germany, and later architecture. By the early 1930s he was married and had established an architecture practice. With his life and career advancing along a comfortable and secure trajectory, the rise of Nazi Germany must have been devastating. In 1934 he was forced to flee his home and, seeking refuge in another country, decided to explore Mallorca. His boat from Barcelona to the island made a pit stop in Ibiza, and Broner instantly fell in love with the island.

Ibiza became a magnet for wartime émigrés, and Broner found sanctuary there among like-minded intellectuals and artists. The local architecture particularly fascinated him, and on his arrival he made an in-depth study of its buildings. He observed, 'These Ibicencan farmers' dwellings constitute a surprise for the modern architect, who is obliged to solve complicated problems of technical, social and functional order, and who is enthused by the simplicity and ease that these countryside constructions present.'

Broner later emigrated to the United States but returned to Ibiza in 1952 permanently and immersed himself in its culture and life. He established the artists' organisation Grupo Ibiza 59, bringing together a culturally diverse group of artists from across Europe. He designed over fifty buildings, many for friends. His own house, which he completed in 1960, combines the principles of modernism with the traditional Ibizan construction methods he had studied all those years ago. The two-storey building with magnificent views of the sea contains the living spaces on the upper floor and studio space on the lower level. Broner lived here until his death in 1972, and his second wife until 2005, when she donated it to the island. Declared a Spanish Cultural Interest Asset in 2000, the restored house is now open to visitors.

Sert Studio

Architect

Josep Lluís Sert

Year

1955

Location
Fundació Pilar i Joan Miró
a Mallorca
29 Carrer de Saridakis
Palma de Mallorca 07015
Spain

miromallorca.com

Two years before his death in 1983, Joan Miró gifted his studio to the city of Palma on the island of Mallorca, where he lived and worked for nearly three decades. Miró had commissioned his friend the prestigious Spanish architect Josep Lluís Sert, one of the founders of the GATCPAC, to design the building in 1955. By this time, however, due to the Franco regime, the architect was in exile in the United States, where he replaced Walter Gropius as dean of the Harvard Graduate School of Design and later set up an architecture practice. As a result, Sert and Miró exchanged plans, sketches and ideas on the design of the building by post.

Miró settled in Mallorca following years of travelling. He bought a plot of old farmland on a terraced slope on which to build a studio, set among carob and almond trees. Miró's brief to Sert was practical: to bear in mind Mallorca's climate and the studio's atmospheric conditions. He also asked Sert to make sure that the work and storage areas were clearly separated. The studio is arranged across two levels. The ground floor comprises a storage area and a double-height painting and sculpture room, bathed in daylight via the high north-facing windows. To the south are large windows that face on to the raised patio, which is surrounded by a high curved wall in local stone. A vaulted ceiling with louvred vents for cross-ventilation and various solutions for sun protection, such as a brise-soleil of terracotta slabs, display the architect's skill at incorporating innovation with traditional materials and a sculptural approach to architecture. The whitewashed facade is juxtaposed with terracotta and the bright red and yellow of the window shutters.

In 2018, structural damage to the building forced the Fundació Pilar i Joan Miró to close the studio; it was fully restored over a period of ten months and is now open to the public.

Casa das Marinhas

Architect
Alfredo Evangelista Viana de Lima

Year
1954–57

Location
Rua 24 de Junho
Marinhas
Esposende 4740–571
Portugal

municipio.esposende.pt

The architect Alfredo Evangelista Viana de Lima fused International Style modernism with the local architectural vernacular of his native Portugal, dedicating much of his career to the restoration of historic buildings. In his own house in the coastal town of Esposende, situated in Portugal's Norte region, he converted an old mill and added a two-storey cubic volume extension to it. The house was completed in 1954, five years after the Charles and Ray Eames Case Study House in California (see page 86), and externally its influences are apparent. Blocks of primary colours are juxtaposed against the white render, and large areas of glazing are framed in blue.

Viana de Lima described his summer house as a 'manor of modern times'. On the ground floor the space is fluid and open, with movable partitions as a way of subdividing the kitchen, living and dining areas. The impressive double-height living room is at the heart of the house, with full-width windows looking out towards the sea. The use of natural materials, such as wooden built-in storage and terracotta floor tiles, provides the interior with warmth and a sense of tactility. The cylindrical body of the old mill acts as the main entrance and stairwell to the upper floor; Viana de Lima even managed to maximise the space by squeezing in a single bed on the landing level. Upstairs the organisation of the rooms in the main building takes a more traditional layout, with two bedrooms, a bathroom and a study with a balcony.

Casa das Marinhas also reflects the modernist programme for outdoor living: large glazed doors connect the building to the garden, which is enclosed by low walls with views towards the nearby pine forest. Meals could be enjoyed al fresco on a built-in concrete table, protected from north winds by a wall with a rectangular aperture. The building is one of several modernist-style houses in the area and has been classified as a Monument of Public Interest. It is open to the public with prior appointment.

Parco dei Principi

Architect
Gio Ponti

Year
1962

Location
44 Via Bernardino Rota
Sorrento 80067
Italy

royalgroup.it/parcodeiprincipi

In the early 1960s Roberto Fernandes, a Neapolitan engineer and hotelier, commissioned the Italian architect, industrial designer, painter, poet and journalist Gio Ponti to design two hotels — one in Sorrento and the other in Rome.

The Parco dei Principi in Sorrento has stood the test of time, and Ponti's original design can still be enjoyed and inhabited as he intended thanks to a faithful restoration completed in 2004 by Fabrizio Mautone. The hotel stands on the site of a former eighteenth-century villa; perched on a cliff between the gulf of Naples and the 65 acres of centuries-old park, it blends in with the surrounding rocky landscape and reaches up to the sky with a tall iron finial.

Ponti, inspired by the site's beautiful landscape and its encompassing blue sky, blue sea and 'blue volcano' (Vesuvius), favoured a single colour palette. He chose to decorate the interior entirely in blue and white: it is adorned with blue curtains, blue chairs and blue bedspreads, and Ponti even tried to persuade the chefs to make blue pasta for the hotel's opening in 1962. A mixture of tactile materials and patterns gives the colour scheme playfulness and vibrancy. Ponti had a love of ceramics and this is evident throughout the hotel, with innovative uses of the material including the ceramic white and blue wall pebbles produced by Ceramica Joo, set into the white mortar, and textured majolica plaques designed in collaboration with the sculptor Fausto Melotti. The theme continues with tiled floors in the bedrooms, where Ponti created thirty different graphic designs arranged so as to give each of the hotel's one hundred rooms a unique pattern. Several pieces of furniture designed by the architect exclusively for the hotel have also recently been masterfully restored by skilled cabinetmakers. The Parco dei Principi is not only one of the first examples of a 'design hotel' but also one of the best preserved.

Villa Necchi Campiglio

Architect
Piero Portaluppi

Year
1932–35

Location
14 Via Mozart
Milan 20122
Italy

fondoambiente.it

Situated northeast of the historic city centre of Milan, the Villa Necchi Campiglio is an elegant rationalist villa designed for sisters Gigina and Nedda Necchi and Gigina's husband, Angelo Campiglio. The wealthy sisters were the heirs of the Necchi sewing machine corporation and well established in the Milanese aristocracy. In 1932 they commissioned Piero Portaluppi, a leading and fashionable architect, to design them a modern home.

Portaluppi designed the luxurious mansion as well as many of its fittings and furnishings. Unusually for its urban location, the villa is equipped with a tennis court and a heated swimming pool —an indication of the clients' privileged status. The clean facade of the three-storey house is clad in coloured marble, stone composite and white marble. The use of expensive materials continues inside, in the brass window frames of the veranda, the walnut parquet flooring inlaid with rosewood, the briarwood doors and the marble bathrooms. On the ground floor, large rooms with high ceilings open on to one another, each with tall windows that give a sense of openness and space. A grand staircase with geometric walnut bannister leads to the first-floor bedrooms and bathrooms, while the attic was given over to the servants' quarters.

The house was completed in 1935; during the Second World War, however, the family moved to the countryside and it became the headquarters of Mussolini's Republican Fascist Party. The British forces subsequently occupied it, followed by the Dutch delegation. When the family finally returned ten years later, fashions had changed and, keen to disassociate the house from the Fascist era, they commissioned architect Tomaso Buzzi to 'soften' the interior, and eighteenth-century antiques replaced much of the original modernist furniture.

In 2001 the house and its contents were bequeathed to the Fondo Ambiente Italiano on the understanding that it would be turned into a house museum.

Ca' Romanino

Architect

Giancarlo
De Carlo

Year

1967

Location
Via Ca' Castellaro
Urbino 61029
Italy

fondazionecaromanino.it

The Fondazione Ca' Romanino offers anyone interested in the work of Italian architect Giancarlo De Carlo or wanting a space for generating ideas for projects a unique 24-hour stay in Ca' Romanino in exchange for a donation to help fund the cost of preserving the building. The house was designed in 1967 by De Carlo for his friends Livio Sichirollo and Sonia Morra, professors at the University of Urbino, as a summer retreat for hosting friends—other intellectuals, artists and thinkers. De Carlo also often stayed here while he was working on the new campus design for the University of Urbino (see page 290).

The house is located about 6 kilometres north of Urbino and stands among vineyards at the very top of a hill. It is reached by a winding track, with its tall, bright red chimney competing with the surrounding trees. It sits partly excavated into the ground, incorporated into the landscape. The dialogue between the house and nature is further accentuated by the use of large full-width glazing in the double-height living room.

The position of the front door is not immediately apparent, and the building playfully forces visitors to weave through a narrow high-walled walkway to its entrance. This sense of fun continues inside, with numerous staircases, ladders and entrances—the house would be the perfect location for a game of hide-and-seek. Its plan is, in essence, an L-shape, comprising a split-level living space, dining room and kitchen on the lower floor, the master bedroom on the top floor, and four single bedrooms positioned in a row in a separate wing with its own entrance.

The central focus of the main space is an enormous red cylindrical metal fireplace, which is echoed by the large round blue metal door that slides open to the landscape in the study. Ca' Romanino accommodates up to four guests, and each bedroom has an enchanting skylight funnel above the bed so that one can look up to the stars at night.

Collegio
del Colle

Architect

Giancarlo
De Carlo

Year

1962–65

Location
University of Urbino
17 Via Colle dei Cappuccini
Urbino 61029
Italy

universityrooms.com

Rooms in Collegio Serpentine
are also available

From the sixteenth century onwards the economy of the once prosperous ancient city of Urbino, near the Adriatic coast in Italy, began to stagnate, and its population declined as people moved away to bigger cities. Due to a lack of investment, many of the historic buildings within its fifteenth-century city walls gradually became structurally unsound. On the recommendation of Carlo Bo, the rector of the University of Urbino, Giancarlo De Carlo began working on a master plan for the city in 1958. As a key member of the Team 10 group of architects, De Carlo challenged the CIAM approach of wholesale redevelopment of cities. Instead, he worked carefully within the existing town fabric, restoring and repurposing buildings that were worth saving.

Carlo Bo also proposed extending the university campus, which would effectively double the city's dwindling population. Mindful that the new buildings should not be located too far from the centre to ensure the city would benefit from the injection of students, De Carlo built the residences 1 kilometre southwest of the city walls atop a steep hill with fantastic views over the landscape. Construction took place in two phases between 1962 and 1983 and the project brought him international recognition.

The first new purpose-designed student residence was Collegio del Colle. It comprises a communal building from which a network of brutalist paths, bridges and cantilevered walkways, responding to the contours of the landscape, fan out down the hill to the 150 private student rooms. The walls throughout the college are in brick, capped with shuttered concrete, the rawness of the concrete blending into the natural landscape. De Carlo designed four further colleges for the university. The rooms are simple yet functional, each equipped with a bed, a desk and built-in storage. Outside term time the college offers short-term accommodation, primarily for academics and students, and is a perfect base for exploring De Carlo's work in Urbino.

Villa K2

Architect

Carlo Mollino

Year

1953

Location
Via Guglielmo Marconi
Agra 21010
Italy

Available to rent via
various sites, including
booking.com

Villa K2 (also known as Casa Cattaneo or Casa sull'altopiano di
Agra) is one of the best-preserved examples of Carlo Mollino's
architectural projects. A mysterious and eccentric figure, Mollino
was born the son of an engineer in Turin. A designer, writer,
architect, photographer, skier, racing car driver and pilot, he
was one of the most multifaceted minds of the twentieth century.
Despite having a forty-year career in architecture, the polymath
has only recently been recognised and appreciated as an
architect. Many of his buildings have been either demolished or
altered beyond recognition. In the last decade, however, Mollino
has gained increasing attention, with his furniture attaining an
almost cult status and fetching huge sums at auction.

An avid skier, Mollino worked on several alpine building
projects, notably the Casa del Sole in Cervinia in 1953. He had a
skill for intertwining the richness of traditional alpine architecture
with the advanced building technologies of modernism, as
evident in the Villa K2. The house was commissioned by the Italian
industrialist Luigi Cattaneo as a peaceful getaway and completed
in 1953. It sits on a secluded sloping site in the Lombardy town
of Agra, benefiting from magnificent views over Lake Maggiore.
The building rises almost naturally from a stone ramp and
stretches dynamically over two reinforced concrete pillars.

Mollino was also responsible for the interior and designed
one-off furniture for it, including chairs in solid wood, bunk-beds
in polished chestnut and brightly coloured coat hooks. The walls
are panelled with Douglas fir, fastened with a rhythm of brass
bolts, while other walls are rendered with a textured, granulated
surface containing shimmering crystal fragments. The floor of the
entrance hall features a mosaic of locally sourced cut and polished
pebbles. Now in the hands of the third generation of the Cattaneo
family, this exceptional house is available to rent all year round,
with accommodation for up to eleven people.

Villa Gotti

Architect

Enrico
De Angeli

Year

1933

Location
22 Via Vittorio Putti
Bologna 40136
Italy

villa-gotti.com

Bologna, the capital city of the Emilia-Romagna region in northern Italy, is best known for being home to Europe's oldest university and for its culinary history. Much of its celebrated architecture, including the landmark Two Towers, dates back to the twelfth or thirteenth century, but there are a few pockets of 1930s Italian rationalism to be found.

One such place is the Villa Gotti, located on the hill of San Mamolo. Its architect was Enrico De Angeli, who was born in Bologna in 1900 and studied at the city's school of engineering, graduating in 1924. In 1925 De Angeli concentrated his career on writing articles on architecture and urban planning for magazines and newspapers; his first published essay was entitled 'Architecture of Tomorrow'.

A chance meeting in 1933 between De Angeli and the local entrepreneur Vincenzo Gotti led to the architect's first and most important commission. The Villa Gotti is a luxurious house on top of a sloping site. Entrance is via a staircase that takes you into the centre of the house and its grand double-height hallway. A staircase leads up to a solarium, and another descends to what were initially the servants' quarters. To the right of the hall are five bedrooms and to the left is a long living room with a statement large porthole window, and a dining room. Not unusually for a house owned by a wealthy Italian family, it also boasts a private chapel. De Angeli designed much of the villa's original furniture, although it has not survived.

After the Gottis sold the house in the 1950s, modifications were made, including the division of the ground floor and first floor into separate dwellings. In 2019 the granddaughter of the second inhabitants, working with the heritage department of Bologna, sensitively restored and converted the house into a bed and breakfast, offering five modern rooms furnished with items appropriate to the period.

Middle East & Asia

The Cinema Hotel

Architect

Yehuda Magidovich

Year

1939

Location
1 Zamenhoff Street
Tel Aviv 6437301
Israel

atlas.co.il

The area of Tel Aviv known as the White City, after the thousands of white International Style buildings there, was constructed between the 1930s and 1950s based on an urban plan by Patrick Geddes. During this era of British rule in Mandatory Palestine, Tel Aviv developed into a thriving urban centre and would become Israel's foremost economic and metropolitan nucleus after the country's establishment in 1948. The whole White City ensemble was made a UNESCO World Heritage Site in 2003. The Jewish architects responsible for the buildings had either studied or been born in Europe but had fled during the rise of the Nazis. They brought with them the trademarks of the modern movement, such as functionality, flat roofs and vertical 'thermometer' windows, but adapted their designs to suit the specific climatic conditions and traditions of Tel Aviv.

A key figure of the movement was Ukraine-born engineer and architect Yehuda Magidovich, who planned over five hundred structures in the city. Unfortunately, many have been destroyed, but one of the surviving buildings is the former Esther Cinema, now transformed into a hotel. With its ribbon-like balconies and concave exterior, the building follows the circular shape of the public Dizengoff Square on which it stands, designed by architect Genia Averbuch. Commissioned by Esther and Moses Nathaniel and completed in 1939, it was one of the first movie theatres in Tel Aviv to offer a truly modern experience. The cinema closed in the late 1990s and was reopened by the original owners' grandson as an 83-room hotel in 2001. The facade, the dramatic staircase and chandeliers in the lobby have all been preserved. Wishing to retain some of the spirit of the cinema and its initial use as a public space, the hotel also screens classic movies in the lobby.

The Bauhaus Center at 77 Dizengoff Street, founded to expand public recognition of the buildings in White City, hosts regular guided tours of the entire area.

Elma Hotel

Architect

Yaakov Rechter

Year

1968

Location
Elma Arts Complex
1 Ya'ir Street
Zikhron Ya'akov 3094260
Israel

elma-hotel.com

Perched high on top of Mount Carmel in Zichron Ya'akov and overlooking the Mediterranean Sea, the crisp white serpentine structure of the Elma Hotel hovers elegantly above the rocky landscape. This brutalist masterpiece and its architect, Tel Aviv-born Yaakov Rechter, gained international recognition as well as winning the prestigious Israel Prize for Architecture in 1973.

The building was completed in 1968, during a time of socialist idealism in Israel and the government's deep involvement in economic and social welfare. Now a luxury hotel, it was once the Mivtachim Sanitarium, a state-run workers' convalescent home intended as a retreat for Israeli public sector workers. The building is elevated on massive raw concrete pillars; the bedrooms were small and humble but with fantastic views towards the sea.

Unfortunately, it was not long before brutalist architecture and the building's modest accommodation fell out of favour as people demanded more luxurious getaways with swimming pools and air conditioning. The Mivtachim Sanitarium managed to stay open for thirty years but finally closed its doors in the late 1990s, after which it was left derelict and with the constant threat of demolition. In 2005, however, Lily Elstein, a wealthy Israeli philanthropist and art collector, saved the building and set about restoring it, led by Amnon Rechter — son of Yaakov Rechter, the original architect — in collaboration with Ranni Ziss. The structure has remained mostly unharmed, with the original timber elements refurbished, the aluminium and plastic cladding removed and the closed-in balconies opened up again. The eighty bedrooms have been converted into forty luxury hotel suites, with additional accommodation in new cottages placed discreetly behind the main wing. Internally the raw concrete walls have remained but the decor has had a contemporary makeover. Additionally, two state-of-the-art performance halls, indoor and outdoor pools and a spa have been added.

Weizmann House

Architect
Erich Mendelsohn

Year
1937

Location
234 Herzl Street
Rehovot 7610001
Israel

chaimweizmann.org.il

The Jewish German architect Erich Mendelsohn was one of the most successful modern architects of the 1920s. The rise of the Nazis in Germany forced him to flee to England in 1933, where he gained citizenship and established himself working in partnership with Russian-born Serge Chermayeff. A few years later he opened an office in Jerusalem and designed an impressive series of projects in British-controlled Palestine that greatly influenced subsequent Israeli architecture.

The Weizmann House, situated in Rehovot, a city 20 kilometres from Tel Aviv, was the private home of Chaim Weizmann, a scientist and later the first President of the State of Israel, and stands as one of Mendehlson's most significant works in Israel. Weizmann commissioned him to design him a modest house, but Mendelsohn persuaded his client to build a grander house at nearly twice the original budget. The symmetrical residence is a departure from the language of the architect's previous work of curved concrete masses and long ribbon windows. The elegant 22-room building is set amid orange groves on an 11-acre site at the top of a hill. Approach to the building is via a winding path around it, allowing visitors to observe the facade from all angles before entering. Internally it is organised around the only vertical element, a dramatic spiral staircase housed in a cylindrical structure, and an inner courtyard with a reflecting pool, which also acts a climatic feature, blowing cool air into the interior.

The villa functioned as the official residence of the president from Weizmann's election in 1949 until his death in 1952. His wife, Vera Weizmann, who insisted on designing the overall look of the interior, lived there for a further fourteen years before she bequeathed it to the State of Israel. Surrounded by the Weizmann Institute of Science, the postgraduate research university Weizmann founded in 1934, the house is now restored to its original condition and lives on as a national museum.

Nakagin
Capsule Tower

Architect
Kisho
Kurokawa

Year
1972

Location
8-16-10 Ginza
Chuo-ku
Tokyo 104-0061
Japan

Tours
showcase-tokyo.com

Stays
nakagincapsuletower.com

For several decades the future of the famous Nakagin Capsule Tower has been uncertain. Lack of maintenance over the years has led to a gradual deterioration, causing rust, damp and perpetual leaking. In 2007, fed up with their living conditions, the residents voted to demolish the building. The construction company in charge of the work went bankrupt, however, and as a result the tower is still standing.

Situated in the fashionable Ginza neighbourhood, the thirteen-storey tower is Japan's best example of Metabolist architecture, a movement founded in the 1960s by young Japanese architects responding to the post-war reconstruction of a rapidly changing society by proposing urban models that were flexible and updatable. The building, designed by Kisho Kurokawa, comprises 140 prefabricated steel cells, each secured with just four bolts to a concrete core. The units measure a mere 2.5 by 4 metres and incorporate a wall of built-in features, including a telephone, a reel-to-reel tape player and a television as well as a bathroom unit and distinctive large porthole window. The units were aimed at businessmen: according to the original marketing brochure, they were 'centrally located to make living and working in the city easier for you. This "capsule" will provide a good living space and a secluded environment in which to select and evaluate business data.' The modules were intended to be easily substituted for new ones once worn out, but four decades later none have ever been replaced. Today only a handful are still lived in, with the majority either empty or used as hobby rooms or offices.

A dedicated group of architectural preservationists are working hard to protect this landmark building, among them Tatsuyuki Maeda, who owns several of the capsules, some of which are available to rent for a minimum of a month. Guided tours in English or Chinese led by enthusiastic and knowledgeable guides offer exclusive access to one of the apartments.

Maekawa House

Architect

Kunio Maekawa

Year

1942

Location
Edo-Tokyo Open Air
Architectural Museum
3-7-1 Sakuracho
Koganei-shi
Tokyo 130-0015
Japan

tatemonoen.jp

On a 17-acre site set in the peaceful grounds of Koganei Park, in the western suburbs of Tokyo, is the unique Edo-Tokyo Open Air Architectural Museum. The compound features thirty restored historic buildings, encompassing a variety of styles and eras, that were no longer viable on their original sites. Among them is the former home of the architect Kunio Maekawa, considered the father of modern Japanese architecture. From 1928 to 1930, upon graduating from university in Tokyo, Maekawa worked in Paris as an apprentice to Le Corbusier, an experience that greatly influenced his work.

The original house was constructed in 1942 during a time when materials were in short supply and regulations forbade the construction of new homes larger than 100 square metres. Despite having a small footprint, the Maekawa House offers a rich spatial experience and beautifully crafted details, fusing Japanese tradition with Western modernist elements. Additionally, Maekawa designed the furnishings and light fixtures. The floor plan is straightforward and centred around a double-height living space, with a bedroom, bathroom and kitchen to one side and a study and maid's room on the other. A wooden staircase from the living area leads to a mezzanine level with built-in display cabinets in wood and glass. The facade is characterised by contrasting elements such as vertical stained timber weatherboarding and translucent screens.

When in 1945 Maekawa's office in Ginza burned down following an air raid, he used the house as both a home and studio office until 1954. In the following years the architect carried out additional renovations and improvements, including reinforcing the foundations, adding diagonal bracing and installing a garage. Twenty years later the home was completely dismantled and put into storage at Maekawa's summer home in Karuizawa until 1996, when it was rebuilt at Koganei Park.

Australasia

Walsh Street

Architect

Robin Boyd

Year

1957

Location
290 Walsh Street
South Yarra
Melbourne
Victoria 3141
Australia

robinboyd.org.au

A leading figure in Australian modernist architecture, Robin Boyd became well known for his Small Homes Service, which he established in 1947 as a programme that sought to popularise modern home design in Victoria by offering house plans to the public for a small fee. His prolific output as a writer and critic secured him an international reputation.

In 1957 Boyd and his wife Patricia bought a plot of land with mature pine trees in the inner Melbourne suburb of South Yarra, on which to build themselves a family home. The site was narrow and awkward due to the proximity of the neighbouring buildings, but Boyd cleverly resolved the problem by dividing the house into two buildings and placing a courtyard garden at the centre. The solution was unconventional and innovative but worked perfectly for how the Boyds lived. At the front, and set back from the street, is a two-storey block designed for the adults, and at the back is a single-storey building for their children. The two buildings share a continuous sloping roof, slung on steel cables.

The house is entered via timber steps that float up to the front door on the first floor. The main living space, with a balcony that runs the width of the room, was used as a living room by day and as the Boyds' bedroom at night. The kitchen and an open-plan family living space were placed on the ground floor and open out to the courtyard. The children's quarters have three bedrooms, a sitting room and a shower and must have given them an enormous sense of freedom.

After Robin Boyd's untimely death in 1971, Patricia determinedly maintained the house, and it remains unchanged, including its contents, from the time it was first designed. It is now the home of the Robin Boyd Foundation, which purchased the property in 2004 to secure its preservation. The foundation offers public and private tours as well as an exciting programme of events.

Rose Seidler House

Architect
Harry Seidler

Year
1948–50

Location
71 Clissold Road
Wahroonga
Sydney
New South Wales 2076
Australia

sydneylivingmuseums.com.au

The architect Harry Seidler was largely responsible for introducing an American style of modernism to Australia. Born in Vienna in 1923, Seidler fled to England during the Nazi occupation of Austria but was later deported to Canada, where he was interned until 1941. Once released he studied architecture in Winnipeg and subsequently at Harvard Graduate School of Design under Bauhaus émigrés Walter Gropius and Marcel Breuer, who had a profound influence on his work. In 1946 he became an assistant to Breuer, assisting on his famous cantilevered Breuer House I in New Canaan, Connecticut.

Meanwhile, Seidler's parents had settled in Australia and urged their son to join them to design them a house. Unable to resist the commission, and with the intention to stay only until the house was completed, he went to New South Wales in 1948. Seidler found a suitable plot on sloping bushland on the northern fringes of Sydney with panoramic views of Ku-ring-gai Chase National Park. The design of the Rose Seidler House is clearly influenced by Breuer, demonstrated in its spatial planning, its setting into the landscape and its use of materials. As in the Breuer House, the entrance and carport are tucked under the raised building. It is divided into two wings — the bedrooms are on one side, the living areas on the other, and in the centre is a terrace with a mural painted by Seidler. All rooms apart from the bathroom have a view of the bushland. Since modernist furniture was difficult to find in Australia, Seidler imported pieces from New York. Internally, a colour palette of contrasting hues is juxtaposed against the textures of natural materials, such as the rough stone walls. The uncompromisingly modernist design of the house gained considerable publicity and Seidler decided to stay in Sydney, going on to become one of Australia's most prominent architects. Today the house is managed by the Historic Houses Trust of New South Wales and open to the public once a week.

Seidler House

Architect
Harry Seidler

Year
1999

Location
Richards Lane
Joadja
New South Wales 2575
Australia

viewretreats.com

Sitting on top of a sandstone cliff with a winding river below is one of the last residential projects completed by Harry Seidler before his death in 2006. The Seidler House (formerly the Berman House) is situated in the Southern Highlands, a two-hour drive southwest of Sydney. It was completed in 1999 for the publisher Peter Berman and his family, who bought the 250-acre expanse of untamed bushland to build a weekend home.

Overlooking the dramatic landscape of the forest and the valleys of Joadja, a steel structure with a concrete floor is set on slender columns, with diagonal braces supporting a projecting deck. The suspended living area is wrapped in expanses of glass. Juxtaposing the location's ancient rocks with modern forms, the house utilises the site's ample sandstone boulders to anchor it to the rugged terrain. With a footprint of 360 square metres, the accommodation is arranged over two levels, with the glazed pavilion of the living area below the upper bedroom wing, and a swooping white roof. 'A level roof would be rather a dull thing to do on such a marvellous site', observed Seidler. 'Thanks to modern technology, we can bend and twist steel like spaghetti into any configuration we want.' The reinforced concrete floors are paved with Alta quartzite, a hard Norwegian textured stone, and the walls are of white concrete block—the materials were chosen for their fireproof quality, enabling them to withstand the devastating wildfires that can sweep through the bush. A landscaped garden leads to a central swimming pool located between two rock cliffs.

In 2009 the Bermans sold the house, and its new owners have converted it into luxury holiday accommodation. With four bedrooms, it sleeps up to eight people.

Image credits

The author would like to thank the following individuals and institutions who have kindly given permission to reproduce their images. Every effort has been made to locate the owners of the picture rights; any omissions will be rectified in subsequent printings if notice is given to the publisher.